The Best Team To Inspire Change

The Best Team To Inspire Change

✦

As Illustrated by: (a) Obama's "Change We Can Believe In,"
(b) Hillary's "A Leader Who Can Inspire," (c) Oprah's "Odds:
Obama 1, Osama O(h)," (d) Patricia II's "We're Guardians
of Obamassimilation" & 50 More Lyrical Poems on Lifelong
Love, Forever Friends

Benjamin Franklin Camins
& Patricia D. Reynoso

iUniverse, Inc.
New York Bloomington

The Best Team To Inspire Change

As Illustrated by: (a) Obama's "Change We Can Believe In," (b) Hillary's "A Leader Who Can Inspire," (c) Oprah's "Odds: Obama 1, Osama O(h)," (d) Patricia II's "We're Guardians of Obamassimilation" & 50 More Lyrical Poems on Lifelong Love, Forever Friends

iUniverse books may be ordered through booksellers or by contacting:

iUniverse
1663 Liberty Drive
Bloomington, IN 47403
www.iuniverse.com
1-800-Authors (1-800-288-4677)

ISBN: 978-0-595-48634-2 (pbk)
ISBN: 978-0-595-60728-0 (ebk)

Printed in the United States of America

iUniverse Rev. date 11/21/08

Contents

Foreword

When I became principal of the Newark Adult School over half-a-dozen years ago, Benjamin Franklin Camins became one of my ESL teachers, and right "from day one" I felt that "there is something about him." I learned very quickly that in fact "there are many things about him," for like Benjamin Franklin of Philadelphia, PA, after whom he was named by his Filipino-Hispanic-Italian parents, he is a modern renaissance man. During his Ph.D. oral examination in the field of History at the University of Toronto (Ontario, Canada), Benjamin asked one of his examiners whether he needed to do an additional doctorate degree in another academic discipline that he was interested in. The reply he received from Dr. Simon Ting, a Chinese-Canadian Professor of Political Theory, was: "No, you simply have to go ahead and do your research in that field, for the Ph.D. that we are giving you today is your license to be an expert in any field of human knowledge."

These are some of the subject fields Benjamin has been considered an expert in:

(1) *African American Studies,* although he is only an African American by affection rather than by race like I am. He and his Burmese wife, Theresa of Yangoon, Myanmar, named their first and only son, Martin Luther King Camins after the most famous African American civil rights leader. He has graciously dedicated to me one of the 52 lyrical poems in this book, "*MARTIN LUTHER KING SENDS ME E-MAILS,*" a rhap (short for rhapsody, a happy and positive type of rap). In it, he has provided the first ever lyric to Barack Obama's presidential campaign theme, *CHANGE WE CAN BELIEVE IN.* He has also included 2 songs for Michelle Obama dedicated to her husband, titled: *I AM PROUD OF YOU & AMERICA, TOO* and *YOU MADE ME VERY PROUD OF ME.* There are lyrical poems about Barack Obama's Kansas White Mom, Ann Dunham; his Kenyan father, Barack Obama, Sr.; his controversial pastor, Rev. Jeremiah Wright; his ardent backer, Oprah Winfrey, and many more.

(2) *Women Studies,* although he is not a woman, like I am. He obtained his credential in Math from the western Ivy-League for women, Mills College, in Oakland, California. The co-author of his first book, *HILLARY IS THE BEST*

CHOICE, Catherine Lien (Vietnamese American), and this second book, *THE BEST TEAM TO INSPIRE CHANGE,* Patricia D. Reynoso (Mexican American) are both his female mentees. He helped the latter to complete her A.A. studies at Ohlone College (Fremont, CA) and her B.B.A. at Cal State, East Bay (Hayward, CA), and he is continuing to assist the former who is just a sophomore at Washington High School (Fremont, CA) in her plan to study Medicine in Harvard University someday. (Previously, Benjamin helped his wife, Theresa P. Camins, to obtain a B.A. in Library Science from Philippine Women's University {Manila, Philippines}, a Pre-School Teacher's certificate from Chabot College {Hayward, CA}, & an M.P.A. from Cal State, East Bay, and he assisted his daughter, Irene Camins-Williams, to complete her M.S. in Biotechnology, also at Cal State, East Bay)

(3) *Mathematics,* the credential he obtained from Mills College. In his Math practice teaching, Benjamin used to be assigned to students who had no interest in Math, many of whom were of the female gender, and before the end of the school year, these hard-to-teach students would become high scorers.

(4) *English as a Second Language,* the subject he taught here at the Newark Adult School (Newark, CA) for a few months short of 20 years. He was introduced to our program in the summer of 1989 during the tenure of my predecessor, Charlie McCrystle, who literally "forced" Benjamin to change his field of teaching from Math to English, provided the latter would take up a subject or 2 each summer toward his English Teaching credential at San Jose State (San Jose, CA). He was chosen Newark Adult School ESL Teacher of the Year in 2000-2001.

(5) *Geography,* which he taught as a Visiting Lecturer at the Graduate Department of Geography, University of California (Riverside, CA) solely based on an article he wrote in the defunct weekly magazine, *Philippines Free Press* (Manila), titled: *"HOW COUNTRIES ARE NAMED"* (July 9, 1968).

(6) *Religious Studies,* in which he obtained 2 masters degrees from Yale University Divinity School, M. Div. & S.T.M. He taught Religious Studies as a North American Missionary to Asia (1980-1989) that included a stint as Academic Dean of the Asian Theological Seminary in Manila, Philippines, and as Professor of Church History at the Evangelical Theological Seminary in Yogyakarta, Indonesia. He now serves as Chaplain of the Society of Asian American Cultural Dancers for Physical Fitness and Recreation, Inc. (*SACSDAPFRI,* Fremont, CA) headed by President David M. Tamayo.

(7) (8) (9) *History, Political Science, & Social Studies,* in which he obtained a Ph.D. for the first field, & a combined A.B. *(summa cum laude)* for the latter 2. He taught them all at the Philippine Christian University (Manila). Benjamin was also invited to serve as that university's president, but he turned it down, in favor of his former Dean at his undergraduate college, Silliman University (Dumaguete, Central Philippines), Dr. Lino Arquiza, a Ph.D. graduate of Stanford, CA.

Law in which he obtained a professional LL. B. degree *(magna cum laude)* is one more expertise of Benjamin, although he neither taught nor practiced it. But, he certainly uses his knowledge of law in his writings and in his capacity as Political Consultant to the Democratic Party. He was appointed to this position, a few days after he became an American citizen on June 1, 1995, by Sen. Dianne Feinstein *(D, CA)* and gave him her direct telephone line to her Senate Office in Washington, D.C.

Dr. Carolyn Scott
Principal, Newark Adult School
Newark, CA 94560
August 8, 2008

Preface

Dear Readers: *(My son, Daniel, at 2)*

I'm a single Mom residing with my son in Newark, CA. My mentor and author, Benjamin Franklin Camins, helped me finish my 2-year A.A. at Ohlone Community College, Fremont, CA and my B.B.A. at Cal State, Hayward, CA. He inspired me to write this song which I sent to Dr. James Dobson, as a possible theme for his program, *Focus on the Family:*

THE BEST OF SOMETHING GOOD

(Chorus:)
I know, I could have avoided
 Being pregnant in the first place
I couldn't undo what I did.
 To loved ones I was a disgrace.

What I could do was look ahead:
 Find something good, and
 make the best.
Your loving support, I do need
 As well as God's forgiving grace.

(1) My child I could have aborted
 Making the worst of
 something bad
Like a criminal most wanted
 Compounded my sin before God
 (Cho.)

(2) My child I could have adopted
 Let someone else fix my mistake
And my problems inherited
 But, my blood I couldn't
forsake. *(Cho.)*

(3) So, I decided to choose life

 To give my own child tender care
Though I'm only a wedless wife
 I'll be his very best mother. *(Cho.)*

PATRICIA D. REYNOSO
(co-author)
 Newark, CA 94560
 08/08/08

Benjamin Franklin Camins *(author)*

FPO

Dedication

BORN TO FLY (To Theresa P. Camins; *Tune:* Cole Porter's "True Love")

(Intro:)

Through all weather
   We never ever fail to try
To give to each other
   Love as high as the sky.

(1) You knew I was yours when you first saw me
   Lovers; lovers
I knew you're mine since I met you
   Lovers; lovers

(Chorus:)

For, you and I
Are like two birds of a feather
   Who were born to fly
Just to give to you and to give to me:
   Love as high as the sky.

(2) And when I pecked at you,
     you allowed me
   Lovebirds; lovebirds
You pecked at me, I allowed you
   Lovebirds; lovebirds *(Cho.)*

(3) The very best of times is yet to be
   Dreamers; dreamers
There's no end to our tomorrow
   Dreamers; dreamers *(Cho.)*

By: BENJAMIN FRANKLIN CAMINS
(06/01/99) 40th Wedding Anniversary

Acknowledgements

(1) *John & Abigail Adams, & John Q. Adams; Harry B. Adams; H.W. Brands; James Buchanan; George H.W. & Barbara Bush, George W. & Laura Bush; Jon Butler; Jimmy Carter; Martin Charnin & Charles Strouse; Hillary, Bill, & Chelsea Clinton; William Sloane Coffin; James Dobson; Al Dubin & Jimmy McHugh; Irene Dunne; Ann Dunham; Dianne Feinstein; Benjamin Franklin* (of Philadelphia); *Billy Graham; Benjamin & William Henry Harrison; Orrin Hatch; Thomas Jefferson; Don Jones; Andrew Johnson; Lyndon Johnson; Joseph, Sr. & Rose Kennedy, Joseph Kennedy, Jr., John & Jacqueline Bouvier-Kennedy & Caroline Kennedy, Robert & Ted Kennedy; Queen Lilioukalini* (of Hawaii); *Abraham Lincoln; John McCain; Charlie McCrystle; Guy & Joni Mitchell;; Richard Nixon; Albert Pennybacker; Cole Porter; Ronald Reagan; Pete & Norita Rich; Hugh E. Rodham & Dorothy Emma Howell-Rodham; LaurieAnn Rosenblatt; Franklin D. & Theodore Roosevelt; Arnold & Maria Shriver-Schwarzenegger; Rick Warren; George Washington, & Shawn Young* (Americans)

(2) *Martin Luther King, Jr. & Coretta Scott King; Barack, Michelle, Malia & Sasha Obama; Carolyn Scott; Oprah Winfrey, & Jeremiah Wright* (African Americans)

(3) *Aung San Suu Kyi & Margaret Pu* (Burmese)

(4) *Theresa Pu-Camins & Irene Camins-Williams* (Burmese Americans), *& Martin Luther King Camins, Patricia B. Camins* & *Merci Mandac* (Canadians)

(5) *Nancy Estefenel; Christina, Miranda, Nathan, & Nancy Jayne, & Joan Venturi* (Chinese Americans)

(6) *Fidel & Raul Castro* (Cubans)

(7) *Paul McCartney; St. Patrick of Ireland, & William Shakespeare* (Englishmen)

(8) *Patricio Albano; Lucas Camins & Crispina Lazo-Camins, Severino & Dolores Tabasuares* (Filipinos); *Raquel Camins; Lyza, Onel, & Eliza Feliciano* (LOE), *Frank & Malou Flores, Louie Garcia, Remy M. Pineda,* & *David M. Tamayo* (Filipino Americans)

(9) *St. Hillarius* (Frenchman)

(10) *Yenny Haryono, Lolo Soetero & Maya Soetero-Ng* (Indonesians)

(11) *Mar. Camins* (Irish American)

(12) *Pope Hilarius I; Gabriella & Mario Tamburrini* (Italians), & *Geronimo*

Ferrari (Italian Filipino)

(13) *Kentaro Shiozuki* (Japanese)

(14) *Jesus Christ & Mary,* the mother of Jesus; *Abraham, Bathsheba, Benjamin, Daniel, David, Jacob, & Nathan; & James & John, sons of Zebedee, & St. Peter* (Jewish)

(15) *Barack Obama, Sr.* (Kenyan)

(16) *Paul Kagame* (Rwandan)

(17) *Edmund Hillary* (New Zealander)

(18) *Erika Perez; Daniel Reynoso, & Angela Rivera* (Mexican Americans)

(19) *Mikhail Gorbachev* & *Leo Tolstoy* (Russians)

(20) *St. Theresa of Avila,* & *Olegario Camins* (Spaniards)

(21) *Thuyen Bui & Catherine Lien* (Vietnamese Americans)

(22) *Photos of Bill, Hillary & Chelsea Clinton; John & Jackie Kennedy; Martin Luther & Coretta Scott King; Barack & Michelle Obama & children* (from Wikipedia)

Introduction

Out of literally hundreds of people who have crossed our paths, there is no doubt that Barack Obama and Hillary Clinton have inspired a change in our own lives best! We have written this book to pass on to you, our Readers, what we have learned about those who have been the inspirational change models in our lives - topped by the best examples of Obama and Hillary - because we think they and *especially he and she can make a difference* in your own lives as they have inspired us to change our own for the better!

The messages of the 52+ lyrics in this book are on *lifelong* love, *forever* friendships, and *deathless* dreams. Obama and Hillary do not only communicate these messages; they have also lived them. They encapsulate the entirety of both their lives and experiences. Because they are universal messages, they are always up-to-date. They are the answers to 3 basic philosophical questions about human existence:

- Where did you come from?
- Why are you here?
- Where are you going?

The respective answers to these universal questions are:

- I came from the life created by the union of a man and a woman in love.
- I am here on earth to make many friends.
- I am going to fulfill all my dreams!

To introduce the parallel messages for change that Obama and Hillary have, and continue to, emphasize, we offer you these first 2 lyrical poems, our own first-time ever lyrical version of Obama's *CHANGE WE CAN BELIEVE IN* and our own proposed theme also in lyrical form for Hillary, *A LEADER WHO CAN INSPIRE*. The messages of both lyrics are convergent in the fact that there is an absolute necessity for *change* and that such a change must come from *bottom up* (instead of the traditional top to bottom), though the emphases are slightly different: Obama, as many of those who have attended his presidential primary rallies, heard him often repeat as practically a mantra that "old-style politics and business as usual of doing things in Washington, D.C. must give way to new-style politics = *change we can believe in*," whereas Hillary projects political change as effective only through a "leader who can inspire us to learn more, to live more, and to love more."

"CHANGE WE CAN BELIEVE IN" (A first time lyric for Barack Obama's theme)

The old-style politics must go
Business as usual won't do
  New-style politics must begin
  A change we can believe in

(1) "You scratch my back, and I'll scratch yours, too"
Is an idea that's quite narrow
  Self-interest we must minimize
  And public interest maximize.
The old-style politics must go
Business as usual won't do
  New-style politics must begin
  A change we can believe in

(2) We must refuse help from lobbyists
They want us to serve their interests.
  As we're the servants of the people
  Our task must be devoted to all.
The old-style politics must go
Business as usual won't do
  New-style politics must begin
  A change we can believe in

(3) Democrats versus Republicans
Is persisting as old partisans
  Remember we're all Americans
  We must work together in our plans.
The old-style politics must go
Business as usual won't do
  New-style politics must begin
  A change we can believe in

A LEADER WHO CAN INSPIRE (proposed Hillary Clinton's theme)

Hillary is a leader who can
    Inspire us to learn more
To live more, and
    To love more

(1)   Hillary inspires us to learn
    About life as a mystery
       Although she had been quite well-trained
    She teaches us very humbly.
Hillary is a leader who can
    Inspire us to learn more
To live more, and
    To love more

(2)   Hillary inspires us to live
    Lives that fully know how to give
And don't only want to receive
    But to share all riches we have.
Hillary is a leader who can
    Inspire us to learn more
To live more, and
    To love more

(3)   Hillary inspires us to love
    The lovable and unlovely
She models her life from above
    Source of truth, goodness, and beauty
Hillary is a leader who can
    Inspire us to learn more
To live more, and
    To love more

Lifelong love, forever friendships and deathless dreams begin at home. All three must be present together. The absence of lifelong love makes forever friendships and deathless dreams impossible.

The home nurtures lifelong love. That is what defines a home. Lifelong love presupposes people capable of loving and demonstrating love right from the birth of a child. As a child is nurtured and loved by its parents so will it grow up to be capable of caring and of loving. A child normally also has other relatives who assist the parents in its care. In some families, the grandma or other female relatives are the default assistant care givers. A new development in family life in America makes the father the stay-at-home caretaker of the baby, while the mother works outside the home! That can only be good for the lucky baby!

The home also nurtures forever friendships. The first best friends of a child are the parents and relatives who take care of it. Then, when other children come, the children become forever friends to one another, too. That is why children who are used to dealing with their siblings grow up capable of lasting friendships in the outside world.

Finally, the home nurtures deathless dreams. The child often dreams of growing up to be like either its father or mother, and sometimes a favorite relative of the parents after whom it might have been named. The choice of what a child would like to be when it grows up is normally to follow in the footsteps of either of its parents and a favorite relative. Martin Luther King, Jr. was a very good example of not only being named after his father, but he also followed him in the profession of a Baptist preacher.

A lot of children follow in the footsteps of their parents and loved ones by pursuing their occupation. That is why we have generations of politicians, civil servants, lawyers, doctors, engineers, scientists, professors, teachers, business people, entrepreneurs, farmers, and so on. Joe Kennedy, Sr., and his sons (Ted, Joe Jr., John, & Robert) and some grandchildren are an excellent example of generations of politicians and public servants. The father and son George H.W. and George W. Bush are another example. In history, the presidential political families include the father and John and John Quincy Adams, the grandparent and grandson William & Benjamin Harrison, distant cousins Theodore and Franklin D. Roosevelt, but Andrew and Lyndon both surnamed Johnson were not related.

Bill Clinton and Hillary Clinton cannot be considered as among the foregoing; they are a category all their own. Hillary was the first First Lady to become an elected official in her own right, as U.S. Senator from New York. Hillary would have been the first wife of a former U.S. president to become president had she won the Democratic nomination and the presidency on November 4, 2008. But, it was Barack Obama who defeated her for the 2007-2008 presidential primary nomination within the Democratic Party.

Not every child follows the occupation of its parents, of course. As the baby finds examples of other jobs, by reading or exposure to them through other media, and even learning about them through practical experience, it may reach out to other equally fulfilling careers. This often is influenced by mentors, who may be counselors, teachers, and pastors or priests.

Though he turned out to be controversial in our time, Rev. Jeremiah Wright of the Trinity United Church, Chicago, was a very influential mentor in the lives of first Michelle Robinson and later when Barack Obama became part of her life, over him as well. Wright was the one who introduced Jesus Christ as Barack's Lord and Master, married him and Michelle, and also baptized their children, Malia and Shasha.

Hillary Rodham before she became Mrs. Bill Clinton also grew up under the spiritual guidance of Rev. Don Jones. She was only 16 when Rev. Jones became the youth pastor of her church, the Parkridge Methodist Church in Chicago, Illinois (too). Her early spiritual upbringing under her mother Dorothy Emma Howell-Rodham as a Sunday School teacher later developed into a Christian social conscience under Rev. Jones.

Couples of the same sex can be considered as having both lifelong love and forever friendships. Because such same-sex union does not normally result in the birth of a child, i.e. a deathless dream, this latter element of lifelong love can be substituted by a child by affection through adoption.

PART I
Love, Friendships, & Dreams
Begin At Home

(Barack Obama, his wife, Michelle, and their 2 daughters: Malia & Sasha
on the campaign trail)

"Teach a child in the way he should go, and when he is old, he will not depart from it." (A Jewish Proverb)

1

Expand "Out Of Many (Backgrounds), One (People)"

"Out of Many, One," the English translation of the Latin *E Pluribus, Unum* is our country's motto. That refers to the multi-background of the American nation that established our one country, the United States of America. Right from the declaration of our country's independence on July 4, 1776, it was recognized that "all men are created equal." The meaning of the phrase was narrower and more literal then.

"All men" meant "all men of property," and Blacks were not among "all men" since the latter had no property and were slaves and by law were themselves considered property of the White men. When our country was founded 232+ years ago, *Out of Many, One* practically meant only White male Americans of Northern European Protestant descent. With the emancipation of African Americans slaves by Abraham Lincoln in the 1860's, African American males became included. It took another 100 years before some Blacks in the southern parts of our country, thanks to the efforts of civil rights leaders headed by Martin Luther King, Jr., did actually practice civil and political rights. And an additional 45 years had to pass before the first viable Black presidential candidate of a major political party Democratic Sen. Barack Obama will be voted upon on November 4, 2008.

The grammar rule that the word "men includes women" did not apply to the original idea of "all men are created equal," for the initial declaration by our founders - who also happened to be all White males - intended the word "all men" to refer only to themselves," and no women! It took another 60 years from the emancipation of Black men in the 1860's for women (both

White and Black) to acquire the right to vote. Thus, only since the 1920's was the proclamation of "all men are created equal" meant to be grammatically inclusive of "women."

"Out of Many, One" was gradually expanded to include Americans of both genders of Southern and Eastern European Roman Catholic descent. It was only in the post-Second World War period following the year 1945 did Latin Americans and Asians (including Australians) become included.

Membership in the body politic did not mean leadership over the entire nation. The U.S. presidency was more of a "White men's exclusive club" that reflected the top leadership in all lower levels of organization, whether public or private. Throughout more than 232+ years of U.S. history, all presidents, including the present George W. Bush, have been *White and male.*

For almost 200 years, only White male *Protestants* were represented in the U.S. presidency. In 1960, *Roman Catholic* John F. Kennedy, made the presidency wider, religion-wise. Kennedy broke the monopoly of Protestants of the highest office of our land prior to his successful candidacy. Despite the fact that he was obviously the most qualified presidential candidate, American voters were so used to voting for Protestants only, that he had to go out of his way to promise that the Pope will not influence his governmental policy. He also took the precaution of choosing his closest rival to the presidential nomination, as his vice-president, Sen. Lyndon Johnson of Texas, without whose backing Kennedy would have lost the close election to Vice-president Richard Nixon!

In 2008, *"Out of Many, One"* hopefully will be wider still, racially, with the election of Sen. Barack Obama as our country's first African American president. As in the time of Kennedy, there have been reservations voiced over Obama's present presidential candidacy. As with Kennedy, Obama with lessons he appears to be following so far, we have no doubt that success awaits him on November 4, 2008!

In this same year, Hillary has "shattered the glass ceiling with 18 million cracks" (the total votes she received in the primary season) in her own words, so that in the not-too-distant future, the top leadership of our country will include one with a female gender, so that she or some other lady can become U.S. president!

Lyrical Illustrations One:

There are 6 lyrical illustrations in this first chapter, with emphases on our being Americans who have come out *"of many (backgrounds), one (people)."* Not only Barack and Michelle Obama and Hillary and Bill Clinton's stories will be poetically described, but also stories of the authors (along with our other inspirers) Benjamin Franklin Camins and Patricia D. Reynoso, in order to show comparison and contrast that of all our hundreds of inspirational models in our lives, the Obamas and the Clintons have been the best.

Lyric #1 titled *I DREAM OF BEAUTIFUL YOU* is a song of Barack Obama to his wife, Michelle. In it, he describes the splendor of 3 places in America that are uniquely connected with his life (a) Waikiki beach near Honolulu, HI where he was born; (b) Chicago, IL, their home city away from Washington, DC, where they currently live to be near Sen. Obama's place of work, and (3) above all, the favorite of North American, even international, honeymooners, the Niagara Falls, NY.

But, even "the fairest view in America" that the Niagara is, in the opinion of most objective observers, to Obama, cannot compare with "the fairest view of beautiful" Michelle! To want to be in a lovely place at any time may just be a dream, but because in reality Obama and Michelle are "destined to be a team," they have "the whole wide world to win."

1. I DREAM OF BEAUTIFUL YOU (Song of Obama to Michelle)

(1) I wish I were back in Waikiki
To float with you, Love, in a dory.
You're with me in Hawaii
Whenever I dream of you
Let's work together as a team
The only right place to begin
"Reclaim the American dream"
And have the whole wide world to win

(2) All roads lead to Chicago today.
Although the roads are countless really,
My own road is the only road
That leads directly to you.
Let's work together as a team
The only right place to begin
"Reclaim the American dream"
And have the whole wide world to win

(3) The fairest view in America
Is the view of the Niagara.
The fairest view from me is
The view of beautiful you
Let's work together as a team
The only right place to begin
"Reclaim the American dream"
And have the whole wide world to win

Lyric #2 titled *HEAVEN IS WHERE YOUR HEART IS* is Bill Clinton's song to his beloved wife, Hillary. It is possible to substitute "home" for "heaven" in the title for they are synonymous. Both places are replicas of the "real heaven where Love dwells." When your home on earth is like heaven, that's "where your heart is." This 2nd lyric traces the many places in which it was like living in heaven for Bill and Hillary: (a) in Yale, New Haven, CT; (b) in Little Rock, AR; (c) in Washington, DC, and (d) in New York, NY.

2. HEAVEN IS WHERE YOUR HEART IS (Song of Bill to Hillary)

When you make earth a heaven
You'll feel at home in heaven
    For, heaven is where Love dwells
    Heaven is where your heart is.

(1)   'Twas like being in heaven
When we met in New Haven
    At the Yale law library
    Where we both went to study
When you make earth a heaven
You'll feel at home in heaven
    For, heaven is where Love dwells
    Heaven is where your heart is.

(2)   'Twas like being in heaven
When you gave up everything
    To spend the rest of your life
    In Little Rock as my wife
When you make earth a heaven
You'll feel at home in heaven
    For, heaven is where Love dwells
    Heaven is where your heart is.

(3)   'Twas like being in heaven
When I became president
    You became my First Lady
    And moved with me to DC
When you make earth a heaven
You'll feel at home in heaven
    For, heaven is where Love dwells
    Heaven is where your heart is.

(4)   'Twas like being in heaven
When you ran for president
    'Tis heaven with you much more
    As our New York senator
When you make earth a heaven
You'll feel at home in heaven
    For, heaven is where Love dwells
    Heaven is where your heart is.

Lyric #3 titled *YOU'RE THE REASON FOR MY LIVING* was the first ever that was written by author Benjamin in the 21st century that grew, along with the contribution of co-author Patricia D. Reynoso, to more than 50 in number in about half-a-dozen years. Benjamin wrote only 1 lyric in the 20th century, and that was *BORN TO FLY* on June 1, 1999, on the occasion of his 40th anniversary celebration with his Burmese wife, Theresa P. Camins, of Rangoon, Burma (now, Yangon, Myanmar) with which he dedicated this book to her (*see* Dedication above).

Sometime at the beginning of June 2002, Theresa asked her husband to write a second song to which he at first objected. But, she insisted, and so he had to. Fortunately, following Theresa's request, Benjamin overheard Joan Venturi, a secretary at the Newark Adult School talking to her husband on the phone, asking the question, "Are you the reason for my living?" It became the basis of the lyric #3 *YOU'RE THE REASON FOR MY LIVING.* At Theresa's suggestion, he also dedicated it to the Camins' ladies and sang it for the first time at the reunion of the Camins' Hispanic-Filipino clan in the USA in Las Vegas, NV in the middle of June 2002.

3. YOU'RE THE REASON FOR MY LIVING (to Raquel/ Camins ladies; inspirer: Joan Venturi)

(1)   No matter where I go,
You keep me company.
No matter what I do,
It's always right with you
        You're the reason for my living,
        You're more than life to me.

(2)   Whenever I feel blue,
You always make my day.
Whatever else I know,
It's all inspired by you.
        You're the reason for my living,
        You're more than life to me.

(3)   Life takes us high or low.
Love binds us all the way.
Our lights will always glow
Till all our dreams come true.
        You're the reason for my living,
        You're more than life to me.

Lyric #4 is titled *"MARTIN LUTHER KING SENDS ME E-MAILS."* Should it not be *MARTIN LUTHER KING SENT ME –MAILS*? No, because e-mails were not invented up to the 1960's when the famous civil rights leader was alive. But, how can the same African American civil rights hero send an e-mail today at the beginning of the 21st century? Read on for the surprising answer.

4. "MARTIN LUTHER KING SENDS ME E-MAILS" (to Dr. Carolyn Scott by author Benjamin)

Teacher rhapper:	Do you know why we have no class on Monday?
Student rhappers:	Because it will be Martin Luther King Day.
Teacher:	What do you know about him, can you tell me?
Students:	He's the civil rights hero of our country.

Teacher:	And that's absolutely right, I must agree.
Teacher rhapper:	Martin Luther King just phoned me yesterday.
Student rhappers:	He phoned? You can't be serious. How could that be?
Teacher:	He also sends me e-mails almost daily.
Students:	But, didn't he die a long time already?
Teacher:	Martin Luther King Camins is my sonny!

Teacher:	(1) When Theresa, my Burmese wife, asked her doctor:
	"When do you think will I deliver my baby?"
	She answered, "No later than the end of this year." (i.e. 1961)
	"Can I postpone delivery to January?"
	"No," she went on, "we can make it come earlier.
	But, we have no technology to delay."
Teacher rhapper:	Do you know why we have no class on Monday?
Student rhappers:	Because it will be Martin Luther King Day.
Teacher:	What do you know about him, can you tell me?
Students:	He's the civil rights hero of our country.
Teacher:	And that's absolutely right, I must agree.
Teacher rhapper:	Martin Luther King just phoned me yesterday.
Student rhappers:	He phoned? You can't be serious. How could that be?
Teacher:	He also sends me e-mails almost daily.
Students:	But, didn't he die a long time already?

Teacher:	Martin Luther King Camins is my sonny!
Teacher:	(2) Come what may, Theresa wanted to deliver
	Our first born baby on Martin Luther King Day
	That way we will be celebrating every year
	Our son's as well as his famous namesake's birthday
	On the first American holiday each year
	We will have much needed rest for our family.
Teacher rhapper:	Do you know why we have no class on Monday?
Student rhappers:	Because it will be Martin Luther King Day.
Teacher:	What do you know about him, can you tell me?
Students:	He's the civil rights hero of our country.
Teacher:	And that's absolutely right, I must agree.
Teacher rhapper:	Martin Luther King just phoned me yesterday.
Student rhappers:	He phoned? You can't be serious. How could that be?
Teacher:	He also sends me e-mails almost daily.
Students:	But, didn't he die a long time already?
Teacher:	Martin Luther King Camins is my sonny!
Teacher:	(3) One week had gone by since the start of the New Year (i.e. 1962)
	I said, "Theresa, for the sake of our baby,
	You must really try very hard to hang in there."

	She went on labor on the tenth of January.
	"Take me to the hospital now; the time is near."
	"Yes," I said, "the fifteenth is just 5 days away!"
Teacher rhapper:	Do you know why we have no class on Monday?
Student rhappers:	Because it will be Martin Luther King Day.
Teacher:	What do you know about him, can you tell me?
Students:	He's the civil rights hero of our country.
Teacher:	And that's absolutely right, I must agree.
Teacher rhapper:	Martin Luther King just phoned me yesterday.
Student rhappers:	He phoned? You can't be serious. How could that be?
Teacher:	He also sends me e-mails almost daily.
Students:	But, didn't he die a long time already?
Teacher:	Martin Luther King Camins is my sonny!

Lyric #5 titled *I'M YOUR IRISH DESCENDANT* enlarges the background of author Benjamin to include an Irish ancestor. Barcelona-born Olegario Camins, the commander of the Spanish garrison in the southern Philippines was Hispanic. Members of the Philippine Camins' clan only thought of themselves as Hispanic-Filipno. "We're Irish, too, and thus true American" claimed author Benjamin. At first, he was not even sure that he was a descendant of Olegario, but he was convinced that he was indeed of a Camins's blood by means of a genetic marker, that is, a straight line across one or both palms of the hand (Benjamin's son, Martin, has the latter).

5. I'M YOUR IRISH DESCENDANT (To Mar Camins by author Benjamin)

(1) I was a plain Filipino
    Born in the southern Philippines
But, I was really bothered though
    That my last name sounded so strange
From all Hispanics whom I saw
    I did not look like a Camins,
My complexion is *mulatto*
    And my feature is Far Eastern
    Once I became a real Camins
    I in turn upset my new kin.
    No Spanish word can end in –ins.
    Anglo-Saxon words have that end
    From Germany, I found "Kamins"
    From England, "Cummings or Cummins"
    We're Irish as per Mar Camins
    Who came years ago from Dublin!

(2) When I came to the USA
    Bing, one of my new found cousins,
Said that she could prove easily
    Whether I was a real Camins
"Open your palms and show to me
    If you've the trademark of our kin
On one palm, a straight line, I see
    Your blood is that of a Camins!"
    Once I became a real Camins
    I in turn upset my new kin.
    No Spanish word can end in –ins.
    Anglo-Saxon words have that end
    From Germany, I found "Kamins"
    From England, "Cummings or Cummins"
    We're Irish as per Mar Camins
    Who came years ago from Dublin!

(3) Theresa, my Myanmar wife, then
    Asked me, "Why don't you look happy?
You should be with so many kin."
    "Yes," I said, "but this disturbs me:
I thought that through a kind Camins

My forbear was his adoptee.
If I've the blood of a Camins,
    I must be a bastard, you see?"
Once I became a real Camins
I in turn upset my new kin.
No Spanish word can end in –ins.
Anglo-Saxon words have that end
From Germany, I found "Kamins"
From England, "Cummings or Cummins"
We're Irish as per Mar Camins
Who came years ago from Dublin!

Lyric #6 titled *ALLOW ME TO BE I* is co-author Patricia D. Reynoso's contribution to this first chapter. It could have been rendered *ALLOW ME TO BE ME* but that sounded redundant. "*TO BE I*" is really more grammatical. "*ALLOW ME*" is okay since here "me" is the object of the verb "allow."

Patricia's background is Hispanic, but it is Hispanic with multiple strains, such as (a) Iberian Spanish, (b) Mexican Aztec, and (c) Caribbean Mix (including Black). She is really the female equivalent of Obama! Like Obama, she claims equality with any White Gringo and Gringa.

6. ALLOW ME TO BE I (Co-author Patricia II's song of multi-racial identity)

Allow me to be I:
    A fully mixed mestiza doll
Born to fly to the sky,
    Espana and Azteca's gal.
Allow me to be I:
    A family's dutiful pal
With a strong Christian tie,
    A Gringo and Gringa's equal.

(1) I'm a true Latina,
    Child of America's Aztlan,
Latin America,
    As well as the Caribbean.
Allow me to be I:
    A fully mixed mestiza doll
Born to fly to the sky,
    Espana and Azteca's gal.

Allow me to be I:
  A family's dutiful pal
With a strong Christian tie,
  A Gringo and Gringa's equal.

(2) I'm a Mexicana:
  I'm stuck with Cinco de Mayo
Sombrero, pinata,
  And the historic Alamo
  Allow me to be I:
    A fully mixed mestiza doll
  Born to fly to the sky,
    Espana and Azteca's gal.
  Allow me to be I:
    A family's dutiful pal
  With a strong Christian tie,
    A Gringo and Gringa's equal.

(3) I'm a new Chicana:
  My husband's mistress and earner,
Queen bee of my casa,
  And my children's pushy mother
  Allow me to be I:
    A fully mixed mestiza doll
  Born to fly to the sky,
    Espana and Azteca's gal.
  Allow me to be I:
    A family's dutiful pal
  With a strong Christian tie,
    A Gringo and Gringa's equal.

2

Winners Name Their Children After Heroes

Psychologists tell us that when a baby is born, it is neutral. But, once the baby is given a name, it immediately starts behaving like the meaning of its name. Next to giving life to a child, the second most important parents can do is to give it a meaningful name. The best way that parents can do is to name their child "after a hero."

Consider what Jesus said about "the greatest love of all" any person on earth can show:

"Greater love has no man than this, than that he should lay down his life for the sake of his friends." That is the real definition of a hero:

H = Help the helpless

E = Encourage the discouraged

R = Recognize the positive in others, and

O = Overcome evil with good, to the extent of dying for it!

Some parents name their child after either of themselves, so that the child becomes a junior, and when junior gives the same name to their child then they end up with a second junior indicated by the Roman numeral III, and so on down the line. Barack Obama and Martin Luther King, Jr. have one thing in common as far as names go: they are both juniors, although Barack does not use the "Jr." after his name as Martin Luther King, Jr. did. Barack Obama, the present presidential candidate was named after his father Barack Obama, Sr., from Kenya. Barack has also a very significant religious meaning, that is, "blessed of God" in Swahili, Kenya's native language.

Martin Luther King, Jr. was actually the second time he became a junior. The first time was when his father was named Michael King, Sr. and he was Michael King, Jr. Many members of his Baptist Church that Martin Luther King, Jr. inherited from his father in Atlanta, GA continued to call him by his nickname Mikey till the day he died.

Michelle Robinson-Obama's first name is, of course, the female of Michael in the Bible, the name of one of the 2 most important archangels (the other is Gabriel).

Another variation in naming their child is for parents to name it after a favorite relative. Benjamin Franklin of Philadelphia, after whom author Benjamin Franklin Camins was named after, for example was named after an uncle who was the most educated member of his clan when he was alive. Benjamin was also the name of the youngest son of Jacob in the Old Testament.

What is the rational for naming children after their parents and close relatives? It has to do with the fact that very often people (as determined by several polls) consider their own parents or close relatives as their favorite heroes!

Parents who prefer to name their child outside of their immediate family also name their children after heroes, who may be religious or secular. Religious heroes are either biblical or non-biblical names. Most religious names are biblical. Roman Catholic saints, for example, are favored namesakes for Catholics. The number one Catholic favorite is Mary, the mother of Jesus. Obama's first-born daughter is also in honor of her, in Hawaiian translation, Malia.

Biblical names may come from the New Testament or Old Testament. The most popular name of previous presidents at 6 was from the New Testament, James, the older brother of 2 Zebedee brothers who were among Jesus's disciples. John, the name of the younger brother of James, was the second most popular among presidential names, at 4.

Non-biblical religious names can include names of Christian saints or famous church leaders, such as Popes and reformers. Interestingly, the name of Hillary in its original Latin equivalent of Hilarius and Hillarius (French variation of the Latin) were both the names of a French Catholic saint and an Italian Catholic pope during the first 5 centuries of Christianity. Hillary, with a double "l" and not just one "l" also happens to be the name of a secular hero, that is, Sir Edmund Hillary the first man – from New Zealand – to have climbed Mt. Everest, the tallest mountain in the world!

Tied at 4 with the biblical name John as the second most popular presidential name is the secular name William. William just happens to be the first name of Hillary's husband, former president Bill Clinton. Bill has a second secular name, Jefferson, the family name of the third U.S. president, Thomas Jefferson, author of the American Declaration of Independence.

Theresa P. Camins, wife of author Benjamin, was named by her Catholic parents in Burma after the Spanish Catholic saint Theresa of Avila (spelled Teresa in Spanish). Co-author Patricia D. Reynoso was also named after St. Patrick, the favorite English Catholic missionary to Ireland.

The other 2 methods of naming a child that parents resort to are: either (a) to name it after a popular place or (b) at the very least, adopt any name with a positive meaning.

Literary Illustrations Two:

Lyric #7 titled *MALIA & SASHA, YOU WERE NAMED AFTER HEROES* is a song dedicated by Barack and Michelle to their only 2 daughters. Barack and Michelle's method of naming their only children follows strictly the traditional Christian way of naming, which shows: (2) they are themselves genuine followers of Christ, "the greatest man ever" and (2) they specifically honored Christ's mother Maria or Malia in Hawaiian translation (since the Hawaiian alphabet has no "r" sound), and Alexander of Macedonia, the greatest military hero in the history of mankind.

7. MALIA & SASHA, YOU WERE NAMED AFTER HEROES (by Barack & Michelle Obama)

(1) We prayed to God in Jesus Christ's name
To give each of you a unique name
As your Christian parents we witness
The Lord inspired us to choose the best
 You are made heroines, not born.
 You are named after 2 heroes.
 They're your guide till you're grown.
 Live as they lived; do as they'd done.
 Just like magic, before you know,
 Both heroines you have become.
 Then someday, when your turn will come
 Name your children after heroes
 And each will become one!

(2) Malia, Hawaiian Maria,
In the Bible, it did first appear,
She was the most beloved mama
Of Jesus, the greatest man ever.

> You are made a heroine, not born.
> You are named after a heroine.
> She's your guide till you're grown.
> Live as she lived; do as she'd done.
> Just like magic, before you know,
> A heroine you have become.
> Then someday, when your turn will come
> Name your child after a hero
> And she will become one!

(3) Sasha, Russian for Alexander,
Its real meaning is "man's defender"
He was Greek Macedonia's ruler
And the entire world, he did conquer.

> You are made a heroine, not born.
> You are named after a hero.
> He's your guide till you're grown.
> Live as he lived; do as he'd done.
> Just like magic, before you know,
> A heroine you have become.
> Then someday, when your turn will come
> Name your child after a hero
> And she will become one!

Lyric #8 titled *CHELSEA, MEMORABLE NAME OF LOVELINESS* commemorates Hillary and Bill Clinton's decision to name their one and only child Chelsea after a hit song by Joni Mitchell titled "Chelsea Morning." It has to do with living in a lovely neighborhood in New York where Mitchell used to live. Guess what? When Hillary and Bill moved to New York from Washington, D.C., so Hillary can begin her term as a U.S. Senator in 2001, Chelsea decided to live in the neighborhood of Chelsea after which she was named!

8. CHELSEA, MEMORABLE NAME OF LOVELINESS (by her Mom Hillary & Dad Bill)

(1) There are places whose names are ordinary.
We went there; so did everybody.
> Please don't ask us about anything we know
> As to what it is, you also do.

You were named after a unique place, Chelsea,
No other name fits you perfectly.
> As your parents your name evokes memories
> When we call, you bring sweet bygone days!

Chelsea, memorable name of loveliness
With you with us, nothing matters else.
> You were our country's First Child yesterday,
> Someday, you'll be our own First Lady!

(2) There are places whose names we don't remember.
All we can think of is we've been there.
> Please don't ask what we saw in particular,
> Because everything is just a blur

You were named after a unique place, Chelsea,
No other name fits you perfectly.
> As your parents your name evokes memories
> When we call, you bring sweet bygone days!

Chelsea, memorable name of loveliness
With you with us, nothing matters else.
> You were our country's First Child yesterday,
> Someday, you'll be our own First Lady!

(3) There are places whose names we want to forget.
We did some things that now we regret.
> Please don't ask us whatever we can recall,
> For, we wish we weren't there at all

You were named after a unique place, Chelsea,
No other name fits you perfectly.
> As your parents your name evokes memories
> When we call, you bring sweet bygone days!

Chelsea, memorable name of loveliness
With you with us, nothing matters else.
> You were our country's First Child yesterday,
> Someday, you'll be our own First Lady!

Lyric #9 titled *MARTIN & IRENE, YOU WERE NAMED AFTER HEROES* is a natural-follow up to the preceding number. This was the only lyric that was authored by both Burmese Theresa P. Camins and her husband Benjamin, parents of their only children, Martin Luther King Camins and Irene Dunne Camins-Williams.

This lyric tells in straight forward language that the African American civil right hero's entire name has become the author Benjamin son's name. Why not just Martin Luther Camins? Because the honoree would have otherwise been the premier Protestant reformer from Germany!

Irene Dunne Camins-Williams was named after the American actress Irene Dunne, who never won the Oscar. But, an actor colleague Jimmy Stewart who presented the John F. Kennedy award on behalf of Caroline Kennedy said that the Oscar should have been given to Irene Dunne, too.

Jasmine was the initial name chosen by Theresa and Benjamin Franklin Camins to give to their second child and only daughter. That had to be changed because Theresa's Mom, Margaret Pu, and other Burmese relatives objected, as Jasmine was too foreign to Burma (Myanmar).

The second choice turned out better than the first. Irene was the Greek goddess of peace which complemented Martin which came from Mars, the Roman god of war. The favorite author of many readers, also, is Russian Leo Tolstoy's masterpiece book *WAR AND PEACE*. The obvious lesson here for some of our Readers is: some second choices can turn out to be better than the first. Do not forget that the name of the African American hero, Martin Luther King, Jr. was also only a second choice, Michael, being the first(*see* the brief introduction to this chapter 2 above).

Just before Irene was to be born on July 20, 1963 in Cleveland, OH, Benjamin's Italian-Filipino step-father, Geronimo Ferrari, wrote a letter congratulating his step-son about the birth of what he expected to be a boy. When Geronimo received the news that the child turned to be a girl, he said, "I'm sorry that she turned to be a girl. She will never become American president." To which Benjamin replied, "Why not? Where does it say in the U.S. constitution that only a boy can grow up to be president?"

Fast forward to July 20, 1969: As a result of John F. Kennedy's space program in competition with the U.S.S.R., Columbus, OH – born Neil Armstrong was near the moon in a space ship with another astronaut, Buzz Aldrin. The Houston tracking station gave them permission to sleep in the spaceship for the night, as they must have been very tired and only land on the moon the following day.

Benjamin in New Haven, CT on the way to migrate to Canada, while his wife Theresa and their 2 children (Martin & Irene) were stranded in Rangoon, Myanmar, remembered praying thus: "Lord God, make Neil

Armstrong land on the moon before mid-night tonight, so that when we celebrate our daughter's birthday, we will also celebrate man's first landing on the moon!" A few minutes later, the voice of Armstrong replying to Houston was heard, "Houston, Houston, give us permission to land on the moon tonight!" And Benjamin said by himself, "Praise the Lord!"

9. MARTIN & IRENE, YOU WERE NAMED AFTER HEROES (by Mom Theresa & Benjamin)

(1) We got your global name, Martin,
From US's Martin Luther King.
As you're both born in January,
Except his is a holiday.
  You are made a hero, not born.
  You are named after a hero.
  He's your guide till you're grown.
  Live as he lived; do as he'd done.
  Just like magic, before you know.
  A hero(ine) you've become.
  Then someday when your turn will come
  Name your child after a hero
  And she will become one!

(2) We got your global name, Irene,
From US's actress Irene Dunne,
Honored in many a genre,
Though the Oscar eluded her
  You are made a hero, not born.
  You were named after a hero.
  He's your guide till you're grown.
  Live as he lived; do as he'd done.
  Just like magic, before you know.
  A hero(ine) you've become.
  Then someday when your turn will come
  Name your child after a hero
  And she will become one!

(3) The Roman god, Mars, you appease,
And Irene, the Greek goddess,
You mirror Tolstoy's masterpiece:
One of the great books, "War and Peace"
  You are made a hero, not born.

You are named after a hero.
He's your guide till you're grown.
Live as he lived; do as he'd done.
Just like magic, before you know.
A hero(ine) you've become.
Then someday when your turn will come
Name your child after a hero
And she will become one!

Lyric #10 titled *NAME YOUR CHILD AFTER A HERO* is dedicated to the triplets, Christina, Miranda and Nathan Jayne, children of Nancy Jayne. They were adopted as *grandchildren by affection* by Theresa P. Camins, the author Benjamin's wife, when she taught them in her pre-school class at the Fremont Christian School, Fremont, CA. She said, "My children were married for at least 10 years; I can't wait for them to give me grandchildren."

Christina was named after the number one hero of Christendom, Jesus Christ, "the greatest man ever;" Miranda was an important character in *THE TEMPEST* one of the memorable plays written by "the greatest English playwright," William Shakespeare, and Nathan was one of the boldest prophets in the Old Testament of the Bible.

10. NAME YOUR CHILD AFTER A HERO (To Christina, Miranda, & Nathan JAYNE)

You are made a hero, not born.
    You are named after a hero.
He's your guide till you're grown.
Live as he lived; do as he'd done.
    Just like magic, before you know,
A hero(ine) you have become.
Then someday, when your turn will come
    Name your child after a hero
And she will become one!

(1) After Christ, you're Christina.
    He's the greatest man ever.
He came to earth from heaven
    So men can live forever.
You are made a hero, not born.
    You are named after a hero.
He's your guide till you're grown.

Live as he lived; do as he'd done.
Just like magic, before you know,
A heroine you have become.
Then someday, when your turn will come
Name your child after a hero
And she will become one!

(2) From Shakespeare, you're Miranda.
He's the best English playwright.
Your name came from Italy,
In *the Tempest* he did write.
You are made a hero, not born.
You are named after a hero.
He's your guide till you're grown.
Live as he lived; do as he'd done.
Just like magic, before you know,
A heroine you have become.
Then someday, when your turn will come
Name your child after a hero
And she will become one!

(3) From the Bible, you're Nathan.
He's a very bold prophet
Who accused King David that
Bathsheba he coveted.
You are made a hero, not born.
You are named after a hero.
He's your guide till you're grown.
Live as he lived; do as he'd done.
Just like magic, before you know,
A hero you have become.
Then someday, when your turn will come
Name your child after a hero
And she will become one!

Lyric #11 titled *'N RICH YOUR CHILDREN'S LIVES* is dedicated to Caucasian American Pete Rich's, Filipino American wife, Norita Rich, *niece by affection* of author Benjamin. They reside in Newark, CA.

"'N rich," is patterned after "'Nsync," a popular contemporary vocal group, simply means "enrich" or "to make rich."

'N RICH CHILDREN'S LIVES

Let it be your mission in life
    To 'N Rich the world's children
Starting with your role as wife
    Then, 'N rich lives of your children.

(1) 'N Rich their relation to the past.
If they don't know their history
Their existence won't last.
They need a beautiful memory.
Let it be your mission in life
    To 'N Rich the world's children
Starting with your role as wife
    Then, 'N rich lives of your children.

(2) 'N Rich their present lives.
To grow up as good husbands
Or wonderful wives
Of great families and clans
Let it be your mission in life
    To 'N Rich the world's children
Starting with your role as wife
    Then, 'N rich lives of your children.

(3) 'N Rich their uncertain future.
To such belong our destiny
There's all we can hope for
If we expect greatness for our country!
Let it be your mission in life
    To 'N Rich the world's children
Starting with your role as wife
    Then, 'N rich lives of your children.

Lyric #12 titled *YOUR SON WILL BE A HERO* is dedicated to Patricia II by her mentor and author Benjamin. It refers to her son, Daniel, also a name of one of the boldest Old Testament prophets, not unlike Nathan. In the Preface to this book, Patricia II herself, a single Mom, also wrote about Daniel in *THE BEST OF SOMETHING GOOD*, a pro-life lyric that she recommended to Dr. James Dobson as a possible theme for his radio program, *FOCUS ON THE FAMILY* (see Preface above).

The tune of *YOUR SON WILL BE A HERO* is borrowed from Guy Mitchell's golden oldie *MY HEART CRIES FOR YOU* whose sad chorus has been completely changed to a happy one:

Golden Oldie:	*This New Lyric:*
My heart **c**ries for you	My heart **c**heers for you
Sighs for you, **d**ies for you	**S**ings for you, **d**reams for you
And my arms long for you	My arms are warm for you
Please come back to me.	Please keep on loving me.

12. YOUR SON WILL BE A HERO (to Patricia II; tune: "My Heart Cries for You")

(1) If you're in Guadalajara, I'll follow you.
If you're in America, I'll be here, too.
I've found a million ways for me to show
My never ever ending love for you
> My heart cheers for you,
> Sings for you, dreams for you,
> My arms are warm for you.
> Please keep on loving me.

(2) Whenever you've to study, I'll support you.
Whenever you need to work, I'll sweat with you.
Your son Daniel will grow to be a hero
Because I'll help you to raise him, too
> My heart cheers for you,
> Sings for you, dreams for you,
> My arms are warm for you.
> Please keep on loving me.

3

"It's Never Too Early To Learn (Or Too Late)"

Education is a continuous process from the cradle to the grave. The earlier a person learns any particular subject such as speaking foreign languages, listening to music, singing, playing a musical instrument, participating in sports, pursuing hobbies, keeping healthy and exercising, and the earlier s/he quits a bad habit, the better!

Obama was into sports as early as his school days. His love for sports such as basketball has not ended even now. He is tall, slim, and keeps his weight down. He also watches his diet. He had experimented with marijuana when he was young, but he has not continued with such youthful indiscretion. The only personal bad habit that he continued with into adulthood is smoking cigarettes, but in this he has substituted his need for nicotine with chewing substitute gum (which his personal doctor has been closely monitoring). Michelle is really the role model for the Obama family in the area of health and physical fitness. She makes most of the decisions about food, eating out, recreation and hobbies for her husband, their 2 children, and herself.

Hillary also tried to be involved in sports early in her life. She even wanted to be a professional athlete at one time, but this did not go very far. She also applied to be an astronaut, but she was told "only male applicants were accepted." The rule had been changed, but not early enough for Hillary to get in. She also keeps a beautiful figure by eating reasonably and in moderation. She could also drink some beer, if the "boys ask her to." She never had any kind of vices. Bill Clinton, for his age as a retired president, has managed to look slim and trim. He oversees his library, and he gets invited to speak. He continues to play the saxophone that he learned to play early in life. He still indulges in his favorite burgers and fries, but infrequently.

Lyrical Illustrations Three:

Lyric #13 titled *I AM PROUD OF YOU & AMERICA, TOO* is a song of Michelle to her husband Barack Obama. Readers will be reminded that this song embodies the strongest rebuttal to the initial criticism in some quarters of Michelle's euphoric remark: "for the first time in my life, I'm proud of my country." Did she mean she was not proud of her country before? Of course not! Even First Lady Laura Bush interpreted Michelle's statement to mean that her "pride of her country is greater now," but that she was "always proud of her country!" Michelle who had learned the hard way, expressed agreement with Mrs. Bush in "THE VIEW" T.V. show.

This incident reminds author Benjamin of his remark to his former English teacher upon her retirement when they met again after a dozen years: "Ma'am, you're looking so good!" Instead of saying, "Thank you," she answered, "You mean I looked bad before?"

13. I AM PROUD OF YOU & AMERICA, TOO (Song of Michelle to Obama)

(1) I was proud of your Mom who was born in Kansas
And of your father who came from Kenya
I was proud of your being born in Hawaii
And when you got your Harvard law degree
  I was proud of you, and America, too.
  I was proud of America, because I was proud of you.

(2) I am proud of our first child we named Malia
And also of our second child Sasha
I am proud of you as my Barack Obama
And for choosing me as their own mama
  I am proud of you, and America, too.
  I am proud of America, because I am proud of you.

(3) I'll be proud when you're President of our country
Or if a president you'll never be
I'll be proud of you when I become First Lady
Or even if I'll be a nobody
    I'll be proud of you, and America, too.
    I'll be proud of America, because I'll be proud of you.

Lyric #14 titled *IF NOT FOR YOU* is Bill Clinton's song to Hillary. It is his personal response to Hillary's theme *HILLARY IS A LEADER WHO CAN INSPIRE* (see Introductory Lyrics above). Be reminded that that song tells us that "Hillary is a leader who can inspire us to learn, to live, and to love" more, more, and more.

Because of Hillary's unconditional love to all, and to Bill personally, and her limitless forgiving attitude, Bill (& you, too) "can learn to laugh, to live, and to love" again, again, and again!

14. IF NOT FOR YOU (Song of Bill to Hillary)

(1) I'd dwell on painful memories,
    Yesterday's misfortunes, too,
And nights of miseries,
    If not for you
Now I can learn to laugh again,
To live again, and love again
These and heaven also,
Because of you

(2) I'd spend all my time daydreaming,
    I've nothing better to do,
Life's rather quite boring,
    If not for you
Now I can learn to laugh again,
To live again, and love again
These and heaven also,
Because of you

(3) I'll have no faith in the future,
  No hope I can hang on to,
And no dreams to die for,
  If not for you
Now I can learn to laugh again,
To live again, and love again
These and heaven also,
Because of you

Lyric #15 titled *A YALE MAN'S ADVICE TO BENJAMIN* introduces Rev. Albert M. Pennybacker, the spiritual mentor of author Benjamin.

It was Benjamin's wife, Theresa, who met him first "under a mango tree in Manila" providentially. And when they met, Pennybacker noticed that she did not look like a Filipina. And she told him that she was Burmese, married to Benjamin Franklin Camins, a young Filipino Christian leader who spoke in her Baptist church in Rangoon, Burma, and whom she prayed to God to become her future husband before he knew her, and that her prayer was positively answered in 48 hours. And then they got married in Manila 3 months later!

And she confessed that her husband gave up his plan to study theology in an Ivy-League university in America to marry her instead. And she felt so guilty about what happened. And she kept praying for God to help her get her husband to fulfill his dream. While pregnant with her first child (Martin), she was now talking to the man who would be used by God as the answer to her second major lifetime prayer, i.e. for her husband to study at the Yale University Divinity School, since Pennybacker is one of its alumni!

15. A YALE MAN'S ADVICE TO BENJAMIN (to Rev. Albert M. Pennybacker)

(1) There was a time a Yale man Pennybacker
  Was going to a church meeting in India
He had at least a couple of days to spare,
  So, he thought he could kill time in Manila.
A missionary friend approached and asked him:
  "If you have nothing better to do today,
Join me to meet leading local churchmen,
  At Philippine Christian University"
He did not know what he could see
He prayed that God would guide His way!

(2) His friend said, "I'm a little in a hurry
     I was asked to preside over the meeting.
So, I'll take my car and drive there right away.
     The place is so near; you can go by walking."
So slowly walked, the Yale man Pennybacker
     Under the mango trees to shield his body
From the heat of the sun in late October
     On the way, he met a strange-looking beauty.
He did not know what he could see
He trusted God to guide His way!

(3) He asked, "You don't look like a Filipina.
     Or, are you from a country I do not know?"
"Indeed, I'm a Burmese, from Rangoon, Burma,
     But, I'm married to a young Filipino."
She said, "My husband is Benjamin Camins,
     Who wants to study at Yale Divinity"
"I desire to meet your husband, Benjamin,"
     He said, "God sent me to help your family!"
He did not know what he could see
He was sure God did guide His way!

Lyric #16 titled *NEWARK ADULT SCHOOL BIRTHDAY SONG* is dedicated to Erika Perez, executive secretary of School Principal Dr. Carolyn Scott. Throughout the nearly 20 years that author Benjamin taught ESL in the Newark Adult School, this song was sung in class whenever a student had a birthday celebration. Two verses come from the traditional *HAPPY BIRTHDAY TO YOU* song and are sung with its usual timeless tune.

What are new about this version of the same song are 2 additional verses that Benjamin wrote that have to do with (a) the language benefit for any adult student of studying English in this school for as short as a year or two, and (b) the extra help that the school extends to its students once they have completed their study program.

16. NEWARK ADULT SCHOOL BIRTHDAY SONG (to Erika Perez)

(1) Happy birthday to you
Happy birthday to you
Happy birthday, happy birthday
Happy birthday to you

(2) Adult School is for you.
Learn English a year or two
  At Adult School, at Adult School
  And speak like a Gringo.

(3) May God ever bless you!
May God ever bless you!
May God ever bless, ever bless.
May God ever bless you!

  (4) Adult School is for you.
  We'll streamline your bio.
  At Adult School, at Adult School
  We'll help find your job, too.

Lyric #17 titled *MY LIFE'S ON HOLD FOR YOU* is author Benjamin's song to his co-author Patricia II that deals with the theme of unconditional care for a significant other, that expects nothing in return because it had all been "paid in advance by others before" as for example (a) Benjamin's Filipina Mom, Crispina, who advised her son "not to ask permission, but to report whom he wants to marry," (b) an Italian-Filipino step-father, Geronimo Ferraris, "who stepped on no one" who helped educate him and his only surviving sister, Pilar, (c) a Chemistry professor and his wife, Severino and Dolores Tabasuares, "who practiced a Christian 'pass it forward' policy since the 1950's," (d) Kentaro Shiozuki, Japanese Asian executive of the World's Student Christian Federation (Geneva, Switzerland), who sent Benjamin to study in London, England, and (e) Albert M. Pennybacker who arranged for his seminary studies in Yale University Divinity School.

17. MY LIFE'S ON HOLD FOR YOU (to Patricia II)

I could have fully retired from teaching
To concentrate solely on my writing
  And have moved to live somewhere
  So far, far away from here
  But, I still have much work to do.
For, my life's on hold for you
  I'm putting my whole life on hold for you.
  Can you put on hold something for me, too?
No, because I'm just passing on to you
What some others did for me long ago.

I could have gone to my Alma Mater
Yale, to do my final book research there
> But, after a year or two,
> What then will I have to do?
I prefer being here with you.
For, my life's on hold for you.
> I'm putting my whole life on hold for you.
> How long will my life be on hold for you?
Till you've obtained the best education
And till your choicest career's completion

I could have married some other lady
From nearby or a country far away
> But, I've promises to keep,
> As you do still need my help.
I may not ever marry so.
For, my life's on hold for you.
> I'm putting my whole life on hold for you.
> Is there something you can possibly do
To show you appreciate my loving cares?
You can put your life on hold for others!

It is a matter of pride on our part as Americans that in 232 years of our country's history, our people out of 43 presidents have had elected 41 who had been married for life! Only at one time did they elect a divorced president, Ronald Reagan. James Buchanan was the only U.S. president who never married!

In the current 2008 presidential election, a vote for Democratic Party candidate for President Barack Obama would continue the 232-plus year tradition of our people preferring a president who believes in lifelong love. He has been married to Michele Obama nee Robinson.

Should Obama decide to pick Hillary Rodham Clinton as his vice-presidential running-mate, she, too, is a strong adherent of lifelong love. She has been married to ex-president Bill Clinton, and remained married to him. Is he a hindrance in an Obama administration? Of course not! The best job for Bill under future President Obama is as a U.S. Supreme Court justice.

Part 1B

Lifelong Love Is Lifelong

(Hillary & Bill Clinton)

[Jesus said], "Have you not read that they which made them at the beginning made them male and female.... For this cause shall a man leave father and mother, and shall cleave to his wife: and they twain shall be one flesh? Wherefore they are no more twain but one flesh. What therefore God hath joined together, let no man put asunder." (Matthew 19:4-6)

4

Lifelong Love Lasts A Lifetime (Or 2)

Both the Obamas and the Clintons are so blessed to remain happily married, otherwise they would not serve as among the best examples not only of our country's leadership but also of Christian family life. Of course, it does not mean that they expect all Americans to become members of their own families' religious denomination: United Church and Methodist Church respectively. For them to want to do that would be contrary to the principle of strict separation of church and state that is enshrined in our U.S. Constitution.

Their strict adherence to the command of Jesus Christ, their own religion's founder, is an example that all Americans can emulate whatever their church affiliation, including those who follow other religions other than Christianity, or even those who consider themselves atheists.

Do their examples contradict those who are of the same sex who get married for life – in some states where they are allowed to marry? What Jesus actually said about marriage is that it is between a man and woman (*see* the quote under the picture of Hillary and Bill Clinton above).

It is not possible for 2 persons of the same sex to marry, for they cannot become "one flesh," the goal of marriage, as Jesus defined it. But, no head of state, including future President Obama can impose any specific teaching of his religion on other Americans.

The exception to marriage as a "lifelong love," given by Jesus, is if one of the parties to a marriage has died, the surviving partner can marry a second time (presumably the survivor can marry a 3rd and more times, if the latter is extremely unlucky!). Theresa, the wife of author Benjamin, a month before going to heaven on July 10, 2002 (due to a heart problem) encouraged him to marry again: "so that you can make some other woman as happy as you made me."

Lyrical Illustrations Four:

There may be many reasons why a man loves a woman, but a golden oldie song with the appropriate title *BECAUSE* rightly concluded that "I love you for a thousand and one reasons. But, most of all, I love you because you're YOU!" Lyric #18 titled I *CARE FOR YOU, FOR YOU,* Barack Obama's Valentine's song to Michelle this year, in a unique way substitutes the overused word phrase *I Love You* with *I Care for You* then gives the reason in a similar redundant sort of way *FOR YOU!*

Barack Obama's love for Michelle enjoins her "to be the best she can be" because the fact that his life is part of her "is the best thing" for him.

18. I CARE FOR YOU, FOR YOU (Obama's Valentine's song to Michelle, 2/14/08)

I care for you FOR YOU.
    Be the best you can be.
That my life's part of you
    Is the best thing for me!

(1) I care for you FOR YOU
    Through the wonderful years
And especially so
    Through rare moments of tears!
I care for you FOR YOU.
    Be the best you can be.
That my life's part of you
    Is the best thing for me!

(2) I care for you FOR YOU.
    I'll always be your friend;
Your real help-mate, too,
    Till my life's very end!
I care for you FOR YOU.
    Be the best you can be.
That my life's part of you
    Is the best thing for me!
(3) I care for you FOR YOU

When you dream your own dream
I'll help your dream come true,
　　　For, we're a winning team!
I care for you FOR YOU.
　　　Be the best you can be.
That my life's part of you
　　　Is the best thing for me!

Lyric #19 titled *YOU'RE MY ONLY LOVE,* Hillary's Valentine's song to Bill this year is a reassurance to him that she is building for him a lifelong "bridge over troubled waters." Whatever might have gone before cannot alter the fact that to Hillary, Bill is *the only one she loves.* To her, that reality will never ever change regardless of (a) multiple transfers of location, (b) myriad alteration of personal circumstances, and (c) menacing threats from a rival or rivals!

19. YOU'RE THE ONLY ONE I LOVE (Hillary's Valentine's Song to Bill, 2/14/08)

Do you know?
Do you know?
Do you know?
No one else
No one else
No one else is the one I love.
Do you know?
Do you know?
Do you know?
Only you
Only you
Only you are the one I love.

No matter where you'll have to go
I'll always be following you
You must know it's true:
You're the only one I love.
Do you know?
Do you know?
Do you know?
No one else
No one else

No one else is the one I love.
Do you know?
Do you know?
Do you know?
Only you
Only you
Only you are the one I love.

No matter what comes tomorrow
And whatever I have to do
You must know it's true:
You're the only one I love
Do you know?
Do you know?
Do you know?
No one else
No one else
No one else is the one I love.
Do you know?
Do you know?
Do you know?
Only you
Only you
Only you are the one I love.

No matter someone else wants you
To share another world with you
You must know it's true:
You're the only one I love
Do you know?
Do you know?
Do you know?
No one else
No one else
No one else is the one I love.
Do you know?
Do you know?
Do you know?
Only you
Only you
Only you are the one I love.

Lyric #20 titled *MERCI, HAVE MERCY ON ME* dedicated to a Filipina-Canadian who migrated to Toronto, Canada from Manila, Philippines where she served as author Benjamin's executive secretary when he headed the National Student Christian Movement of the Philippines.

Her name was one of the ladies Theresa recommended in her diary that she left with her daughter Irene, to be handed to her Dad so that the latter could explore someone "to take her (Theresa's) place when she would have gone to heaven."

20. MERCI, HAVE MERCY ON ME (to Merci Mandac)

Just before Theresa went to heaven,
She chose you among the few women
    Who could take her place as my loving wife
    All the rest of my life:
She thought that you represent the country
She stole me from on marrying me.
    She is restoring me to you, Mercy.
    Will you please marry me?

(1) But, you said that you're against having me
    For, you're committed to another.
Although you're not married in reality,
    You have lived together.
Just before Theresa went to heaven,
She chose you among the few women
    Who could take her place as my loving wife
    All the rest of my life:
She thought that you represent the country
    She stole me from on marrying me.
She is restoring me to you, Mercy.
    Will you please marry me?

(2) A stroke had overtaken your lover.
    To marry me wasn't your desire.
Because now, he needs you more than ever
    Your choice I do admire.
Just before Theresa went to heaven,
    She chose you among the few women

Who could take her place as my loving wife
     All the rest of my life:
She thought that you represent the country
     She stole me from on marrying me.
She is restoring me to you, Mercy.
     Will you please marry me?

(3) I didn't mean to take you away from him.
     I desire to marry you only
So I can help you to take care of him.
     But, you said, "That's crazy!"

Lyric #21 titled *I'VE ALWAYS LOVED YOU AS MY DAUGHTER* is dedicated to Yenny Haryono, the official hostess when author Benjamin and Theresa served as North American missionaries assigned to the Evangelical Theological Seminary in Yogyakarta, Indonesia. It was Theresa's idea to adopt her as *her daughter by affection* with the idea of recommending her to her son, Martin Luther King Camins to marry. God had another plan for Martin who married Patricia I Bordon of Waterloo, Ontario, Canada.

Yenny's name was included by Theresa in her list in the diary that she left with Irene to be handed over to her Dad, after her Mom would have gone to be with Jesus in heaven. Did Benjamin have better luck with Yenny than with Merci?

21. I'VE ALWAYS LOVED YOU AS MY DAUGHTER (to Yenny Haryono)

(1) If I should live to be a hundred,
     I pledge 35 years of faithfulness.
About nothing, you have to be scared.
     God knows you deserve all blessedness.
I've always loved you, as my daughter.
     I'll love you even more as my wife.
My love for you will last forever
     No matter how short will be my life.

(2) If I should live till I reach ninety,
    I vow 25 years of devotion.
I'll always make you very happy
    Till the end of our divine mission
I've always loved you, as my daughter.
    I'll love you even more as my wife.
My love for you will last forever
    No matter how short will be my life.

(3) If I should live till I reach eighty,
    Just 15 years together seems unfair.
That's 15 years more than anybody
    Who's fated not to marry ever.
I've always loved you, as my daughter.
    I'll love you even more as my wife.
My love for you will last forever
    No matter how short will be my life

Lyric #22 titled *MY UNSTOPPABLE LOVE FOR YOU* is dedicated by Benjamin to his co-author, Patricia II. Do you think that there is something other than "Platonic love" going on between them?

22. MY UNSTOPPABLE LOVE FOR YOU (to Patricia II)

(1) If they take you to a place so far away,
    They can't stop my unstoppable love for you.
I'll count the days till you're home again with me.
    My heart won't rest till it rests once more in you!
Nothing can stop my unstoppable love for you.
    Not distance: It'll only make my heart grow fonder.
Not prison: I'll break any prison wall for you.
    Not death: I'll be your special angel forever!

(2) If they cast my body in any prison,
    They can't stop my unstoppable love for you.
No suffering can ever be a reason
    To change my feelings of being close to you!
Nothing can stop my unstoppable love for you.
    Not distance: It'll only make my heart grow fonder.
Not prison: I'll break any prison wall for you.
    Not death: I'll be your special angel forever!

(3) If they drive my life to an untimely end,
    They can't stop my unstoppable love for you.
I'll meet my other love, Theresa, in heaven,
    And she and I will lovingly wait for you!
Nothing can stop my unstoppable love for you.
    Not distance: It'll only make my heart grow fonder.
Not prison: I'll break any prison wall for you.
    Not death: I'll be your special angel forever!

5

There's No Wrong Forgiveness Cannot Cure

We think that one of the major causes of divorce in the United States is not because there is so much freedom. That is not as serious a cause as lack of forgiveness of the offender by the offended party in a marriage. Barack and Michelle Obama's marriage, they will be the first to admit, is far from perfect. Nevertheless, in spite of their differences and disagreements, they have learned as practicing Christians to resort to the exact reverse side of unconditional love, which is unlimited forgiveness.

In the case of Hillary, the agonies she had gone through because of Bill, her husband while president, had affairs with few other women. That articles of impeachment were brought against him in the U.S. House of Representatives, although he was not convicted by the U.S. Senate, is public knowledge.

Of 2 alternatives available to Hillary: to divorce or to stay with her husband, she chose the latter. She chose to stand by her man. She could have divorced Bill, as some of her friends advised her; she decided to forgive him. Her motive was criticized as a sign of ambitiousness on her part: that her future chance at winning the U.S. presidency will be jeopardized. One proof can overthrow this line of thinking right away. A once-divorced person is not automatically disqualified from becoming president. President Ronald Reagan, the lone example among previous presidents, had shown that his one-divorce was not a barrier to his becoming U.S. president.

In any case, Hillary at this writing is no longer the nominee of the Democratic Party in this year's election, but Barack Obama. Lo and behold, Hillary is still standing by her man!

Lyrical Illustrations Five:

Lyric #23 titled *YOU'RE MORE THAN LOVE TO ME* is both a song of Barack Obama to Michelle, and of Bill to Hillary Clinton. Both ladies, to a greater or less degree, have been wonderful to their respective husbands. Whatever wrongs each of the gentlemen, to a greater or less degree, to their respective wives, the latter had forgiven them.

In the Bible one finds that "forgiveness covers a multitude of sins." When Jesus was asked by Peter how many times must he forgive someone who wronged him, "Seven times?" Jesus replied: "No, seven times seventy times," which is to say, "it is unlimited!"

23. YOU'RE MORE THAN LOVE TO ME (to Michelle by Obama, & to Hillary by Bill)

(1) Oh, you're so wonderful!
     None can compare with you
I can act like a fool
     I've your permission to.
When I'm wrong, you forgive.
     You're the cause I survive.
You've taught me how to live
     I'm glad to be alive.
You're more than love to me
And I'm yours eternally

(2) We're opposites, it's said,
     Like lemon and water.
But, we're sweet lemonade
     When we work together
When I'm wrong, you forgive.
     You're the cause I survive.
You've taught me how to live
     I'm glad to be alive.
You're more than love to me
And I'm yours eternally

(3) We've not always agreed
    On all things, but somehow
When it really mattered,
    There's always a way how.
When I'm wrong, you forgive.
    You're the cause I survive.
You've taught me how to live
    I'm glad to be alive.
You're more than love to me
And I'm yours eternally

Lyric #24 titled *PLEASE DON'T HOLD YESTERDAY AGAINST ME* is Obama's song asking his supporters to forgive his past associations without limits: (a) whatever he might done, or (b) whatever he might have left undone, or (c) whether he had lost or won, or (d) whether he had pain or fun.

His plea for forgiveness is based on the reality that: (a) "yesterday was long ago," and (b) "yesterday is gone!"

24. PLEASE DON'T HOLD YESTERDAY AGAINST ME
(Obama's Plea)

(1) Please don't hold yesterday against me
    No matter what I might have done.
For, yesterday was long ago
    And yesterday is gone!
Why worry about Jeremiah Wright
    When as African American
He preached about what he thought were right
    I could still respect him as a man.

(2) Please don't hold yesterday against me
    No matter what I've left undone.
For, yesterday was long ago
    And yesterday is gone.
Why didn't I leave Wright's Trinity Church,
    Since I had twenty years to decide?
Wright led me to Jesus and my faith
    He wed me and my children baptized.

(3) Please don't hold yesterday against me
        No matter we had lost or won
For, yesterday was long ago
        And yesterday is gone.
But, when Pastor Wright had repeated
        "That our government had intended
Black Americans be infected
        With HIV," "That's nonsense," I said.

(4) Please don't hold yesterday against me
        No matter we've had pain or fun.
For, yesterday was long ago
        And yesterday is gone.
The last straw came when Pfleger did preach
        At the United Trinity Church:
"Hillary thinks she deserves to win
        For, white is the color of her skin."

Lyric #25 titled *I WON'T HOLD YESTERDAY AGAINST YOU* is the exact reverse of lyric #24 and it is a song of forgiveness of Hillary to Bill for (a) whatever he had done, (b) had left undone, or (c) whether he had pain or fun.

She gives 2 additional reasons why she is able to forgive Bill apart from the fact that (a) "yesterday was long ago" and (b) "yesterday is gone." (c) Today, "there are lots of things to do," and (d) tomorrow, "there's a whole lifetime to go."

25. I WON'T HOLD YESTERDAY AGAINST YOU
(Hillary forgave Bill)

(1) I won't hold yesterday against you
        No matter what you might have done.
For, yesterday was long ago
        And yesterday is gone!
Why resurrect the dead past today
        When there are lots of things to do
With your head high come what may
        The present is all you've to go through.

Why have regrets about yesterday
    When there's still a whole life-time to go?
While alive there'll be a better day,
    And there's always hope for tomorrow!

(2) I won't hold yesterday against you
    No matter what you've left undone.
For, yesterday was long ago
    And yesterday is gone.
Why resurrect the dead past today
    When there are lots of things to do
With your head high come what may
    The present is all you've to go through.
Why have regrets about yesterday
    When there's still a whole life-time to go?
While alive there'll be a better day,
    And there's always hope for tomorrow!

(3) I won't hold yesterday against you
    No matter we've had pain or fun.
For, yesterday was long ago
    And yesterday is gone.
Why resurrect the dead past today
    When there are lots of things to do
With your head high come what may
    The present is all you've to go through.
Why have regrets about yesterday
    When there's still a whole life-time to go?
While alive there'll be a better day,
    And there's always hope for tomorrow!

Lyric #26 titled *YOU WERE MY SWEETEST SONG* is author Benjamin's song of forgiveness for Angela of Bakersfield, CA. After Mercy Mandac and Yenny Haryono had turned down his proposal to marry as suggested by Theresa in a notebook left with their daughter, Irene, Benjamin met Angela in Newpark Mall, Newark, CA, and he thought she might be "the woman whom he can make as happy as he had made Theresa" for 42 years.

Should the song have been titled *YOU **ARE** MY SWEETEST SONG?*

26. YOU WERE MY SWEETEST SONG
(Benjamin forgave Angela)

You said you love my songs.
  With that, there's nothing wrong.
But, with each of my songs,
  I completely belong.
And you can't love my songs,
  Unless I tug along!

(1) Would you love my songs without me?
  Would you love me without a song?
I beg you: love my songs with me,
  As well as love me with my songs.
You said you love my songs.
  With that, there's nothing wrong.
But, with each of my songs,
  I completely belong.
And you can't love my songs,
  Unless I tug along!

(2) For, all my songs are all me
  And all of me is all my songs.
You can only have all of me
  When you will have all of my songs
You said you love my songs.
  With that, there's nothing wrong.
But, with each of my songs,
  I completely belong.
And you can't love my songs,
  Unless I tug along!

(3) I used to sing you my old songs
  My newest song is all of you.
You're the sweetest of all my songs,
  And my best song of all is you!
You said you love my songs.
  With that, there's nothing wrong.

But, with each of my songs,
    I completely belong.
And you can't love my songs,
    Unless I tug along!

(4) You're also my very last song.
    My inspiration died with you.
I'll never write another song
    Till you love me as I love you!

Lyric #27 titled *TODAY* is dedicated to Benjamin by his co-author Patricia II. This song contrasts with the Paul McCartney's *YESTERDAY* which is nostalgic, and with Martin Charnin & Charles Strouse's *TOMORROW,* orphan Annie's song in the Broadway musical *ANNIE,* which is futuristic. This lyric *TODAY* has a Christian existentialist point of view in that Patricia II is content with the joy of being loved today because (a) "yesterday cannot be brought to life again" (a dead past) and (b) "tomorrow is so uncertain" (a big gamble).

27. TODAY (to Benjamin by Patricia II)

I don't know what tomorrow brings.
I don't care for what might have been.
I want to be sure that today
Your love alone does count for me

(1) Tomorrow is so uncertain.
We can plan a few little things.
And hope and pray that all the rest
Will still turn out to be the best!
I don't know what tomorrow brings.
I don't care for what might have been.
I want to be sure that today
Your love alone does count for me

(2) Yesterday's unique achievements
And yesterday's undeserved pains
Cannot be brought to life again
We thank God for all we did learn
I don't know what tomorrow brings.
I don't care for what might have been.
I want to be sure that today
Your love alone does count for me

(3) Today is time fully to live
And to love, to serve, and to give
To hurt, and forgiveness receive.
Or to be hurt, and to forgive!
I don't know what tomorrow brings.
I don't care for what might have been.
I want to be sure that today
Your love alone does count for me

6

Successful People Have Supportive Significant Others

We have chosen the phrase "significant others" in this chapter's title instead of the traditional "woman" or less traditional "spouse" because the phrase could mean both "the woman behind the man" (Michelle behind Barack Obama) and "the man behind the woman" (Bill behind Hillary Clinton). "Significant others" can also include non-marital close relationships, and of course, it can include multiple close relationships.

That Michelle is strongly supportive of Barack Obama her husband is obvious. She is as qualified as he in all aspects of background, education, and job experiences. She was even ahead of him in one way: she started as Barack Obama's mentor in Chicago in his first law firm.

She would have had the priority to run for president, if she were a man. But, she was willing to subordinate all that to be "the woman behind her man."

Hillary, too, has stood by her man. If that were just one-sided, then the marriage would not have lasted. You might find this hard to believe, but Bill has decided to reciprocate her love! How did Hillary know, if she had doubts about her affection before, because of those other women in his life. She wanted to reassure herself somehow.

And Bill came out with flying colors! What did he do that made Hillary realize that his love for her is genuine? That was when Bill, who was addicted to 2 major things (1) eating junk food and (2) watching the football super bowl game every year. For the first time, in January 2008, Bill had to miss watching the superbowl game, in order to go campaigning for her in Iowa.

Author Benjamin wrote the most number of love songs for his co-author Patricia II. He hopes that someday she'll say she loves him. She does not allow him to say to her, "I love you." .

Lyrical Illustrations Six:

Lyric #28 titled *"YOU MADE ME VERY PROUD OF ME"* is a song of self-esteem of Michelle to her husband, Barack. There had been 4 coincidences that could have prevented Barack from becoming the husband of Michelle: he could have married (a) a Hawaiian lady, "Leilani" being the most popular name for a girl in the islands, or (b) a Brown lady from the island of Java, Indonesia, or (c) a White lady since his Mom, Ann Dunham, happened to be of that race, or (d) another Black lady from another country, Kenya, his own father's place of birth.

We do not believe coincidences are merely accidental, however, especially when they are multiple rather just one. The better explanation for people of Christian persuasion is that it's no less than a "God-given destiny" that Michelle Robinson of Chicago, IL, became the one and only love of Barack Obama. Why? From a human point of view, there were equally compelling coincidences: (a) they share blackness as a color of their skin; (b) they enjoyed scholarships when they went through undergraduate degrees in 2 Ivy-league universities, Columbia and Princeton respectively; (c) they both took up a degree in law from the number one Ivy-League university, Harvard; (d) they attended the same church, the Trinity United Church of Christ, Chicago, IL, and (e) they worked in the same Chicago law office.

28. YOU MADE ME VERY PROUD OF ME (Song of Michelle to Barack Obama)

(1) You could have stayed in Hawaii
Where you first saw the light of day
You could have wed a "Leilani"
And raised an island family
    But that was never meant to be
    It's our God-given destiny
    To fall in love and to marry
    You made me very proud of me.

(2) You could have moved to Indonesia
When your Mom lived in Jakarta
You could have spoken Bahasa

And wed a lady from Java.
> But that was never meant to be
> It's our God-given destiny
> To fall in love and to marry
> You made me very proud of me.

(3) You could have wed a White lady
Like Ann Dunham, your own Mommy,
Settled in Kansas all your days
We would have had separate ways
> But that was never meant to be
> It's our God-given destiny
> To fall in love and to marry
> You made me very proud of me.

(4) You could have followed your Papa
When he returned to Africa
Bade farewell to America
And wed a lady from Kenya
> But that was never meant to be
> It's our God-given destiny
> To fall in love and to marry
> You made me very proud of me.

Lyric #29 titled *MY BEST GIFT TO YOU* is Bill's song to Hillary on her 60th birthday, October 26, 2007. Whatever gift Bill gave to her on that day he has not revealed to us, but that does not matter. For, as the truly supportive man behind her woman in the words of the song, "the best gift for you from me is the gift of me everyday!"

29. MY BEST GIFT TO YOU
(Song of Bill to Hillary on her 60th birthday)

I'm giving you a gift today.
No matter what that gift may be.
For the best gift for you from me
Is the gift of me everyday!

(1) I love you with my entire life on earth.
If allowed, I'll love you more after death.
> Although our celebrations abound

Count on me always to be around!
I'm giving you a gift today.
No matter what that gift may be.
For the best gift for you from me
Is the gift of me everyday!

(2) I befriend you with fondness forever.
We'll share our joys and sorrows together.
All of our loved ones will feel welcome,
So will our old and new friends, at home.
I'm giving you a gift today.
No matter what that gift may be.
For the best gift for you from me
Is the gift of me everyday!

(3) I dream with you a dream that is deathless.
That each day people will find real peace
That no children die prematurely,
Or survive and suffer needlessly!
I'm giving you a gift today.
No matter what that gift may be.
For the best gift for you from me
Is the gift of me everyday!

Lyric #30 titled *YOU'RE MY BUNNY BENNY* is co-author Patricia II's song to Benjamin as the first "significant other" of the latter. Of all the possible alternatives (a) his matching her to some other gentleman, (b) his wanting to marry her, (c) his adopting her, or (d) her remaining "a forever friend who loves him to the end," she preferred the last one.

30. YOU'RE MY BUNNY BENNY
(to Benjamin by Patricia II)

(1) First, you tried to match me
     With someone you well know.
He's more problem to me
     Than I already do.
By birth, you're Benjamin.
You prefer to be Ben.
Your friends call you Bengie,
To me, you're Bunny Benny.

(2) Then, you said if need be,
     You'll even marry me.
But, that can't ever be,
     If you won't live with me
By birth, you're Benjamin.
You prefer to be Ben.
Your friends call you Bengie,
To me, you're Bunny Benny.

(3) Why not try one more way?
     Please adopt me for you.
But, I'm not a baby.
     I can't grow up with you.
By birth, you're Benjamin.
You prefer to be Ben.
Your friends call you Bengie,
To me, you're Bunny Benny.

(4) Still, throughout all my life,
     You'll always be my friend.
Not as daughter or wife,
     I'll love you to the end!
By birth, you're Benjamin.
You prefer to be Ben.
Your friends call you Bengie,
To me, you're Bunny Benny.

Lyric #31 titled *HEAVEN IS LIVING WITH TINA* is dedicated to
Thuyen Bui, Vietnamese-American roommate of author Benjamin. Besides

her being a "significant other" of Benjamin, she also serves as his lifetime barber-hairdresser and housekeeper. She is the aunt of the Harvard-bound high school girl, Catherine Lien, featured in lyric #50.

31. HEAVEN IS LIVING WITH TINA
(Dedicated to Thuyen Bui)

Whatever else I can say,
Or can ever hope to be,
One thing is quite sure to me,
Heaven's living with Tina.

(1) Once I didn't know where to go,
Or what else I had to do,
Tina came to my rescue
And then gave me heaven, too.
Whatever else I can say,
Or can ever hope to be,
One thing is quite sure to me,
Heaven's living with Tina.

(2) She said, "No need to worry
To face this or any day,
Because you can always stay,
You can come and live with me."
Whatever else I can say,
Or can ever hope to be,
One thing is quite sure to me,
Heaven's living with Tina.

(3) I've no riches to share her,
I'm not handsome to please her,
I'm not young and strong for her,
Yet, she treats me with tender care.
Whatever else I can say,
Or can ever hope to be,
One thing is quite sure to me,
Heaven's living with Tina.

Lyric #32 *FLOAT OFF ON A CLOUD* is dedicated to LaurieAnne Rosenblatt, former co-teacher of author Benjamin in ESL at the Newark Adult

School, Newark, CA. Besides being another "significant other" of Benjamin, she has agreed to co-author with him, one of the B.E.S.T. (Basic Expositions - on - Selected Topics) books in the near future: *THE BEST WAY TO LEARN ENGLISH.* She once complained that Benjamin wrote many lyrics dedicated to others, "Why did you not write more than one for me?" He answered, "It's not quantity but quality that counts." *FLOAT OFF ON A CLOUD* happens to be the number 1 favorite of Newark Adult ESL students.

32. FLOAT OFF ON A CLOUD
(to LaurieAnne Rosenblatt)

(1) There are a million things to do.
    There's never enough time to rest.
End a job; one more follows you.
    And you can't float off on a cloud just yet.
Someday, the situation will change.
Someday, the sun will keep shinin'.
    Gray skies turn blue; and dark clouds, white.
    You can float off on a cloud all you wish!

(2) There might be a past to undo.
    Regrets you must need to forget.
Forgiveness for wrongs done to you
    So, you can't float off on a cloud just yet.
Someday, the situation will change.
Someday, the sun will keep shinin'.
    Gray skies turn blue; and dark clouds, white.
    You can float off on a cloud all you wish!

(3) There may be plans you must forego.
    Remove some world's cares from your net.
Have a load light enough for you.
    Still, you can't float off on a cloud just yet.
Someday, the situation will change.
Someday, the sun will keep shinin'.
    Gray skies turn blue; and dark clouds, white.
    You can float off on a cloud all you wish!

If lifelong love is not possible for any reason, forever friendship is an ideal alternative. After all, it is not possible for anyone one person to marry more than one. That is, of course, according to the standard of monogamy required by Jesus of his followers.

The number of forever friends one can have is unlimited. Friends can, of course, be shorter than forever. The friends of childhood may not continue in adulthood. Our friends in pre-school may not continue in elementary school, high school, college, and at work. As human beings, we tend to move a lot.

Likewise, we have friends in different places at the same time: our friends at school are different from our friends at church and different again from our friends at work or even friends at leisure!

The purpose of human life on earth is to make friends. It can be a synonym for patriotism. It can be equated to love of our country, even dying for it. After all, a country is really the geographical boundary of a people or nation who desire to live together. It is not as important to live long lives, as to live so as to make a difference in the lives of others. That is what we mean by leaving a legacy before we go to heaven.

Of all U.S. presidents in American history, it was John F. Kennedy who can be remembered most for his challenge to his and future generations to be involved in public service:

"Ask what you can do for your country, not what your country can do for you." Or,

"Ask what you can do for your people, not what your people can do for you." Or,

"Ask what you can do for your friends, not what your friends can do for you."

PART 2

Forever Friends Are Friends Forever

(President John F. Kennedy & his wife, Jackie, greeting a political supporter)

"Ask not what your country can do for you; ask what you can do for your country." (John F. Kennedy)

7

"It Takes 2 (Ivy-Leaguers) To Tango"

"It takes 2 to tango." It takes 2 to dance any ballroom dance such as cha-cha, waltz, rumba, fox trot, 2-step, salsa, mambo, meringue, twist, rock & roll, jitterbug, etc. It takes 2 to dance gracefully. These are illustrative of a political winning combination.

One ivy-leaguer, Obama or Hillary, can be good enough to win the presidency. During the primary season, both Obama and Hillary had energized the Democratic base. Obama had drawn younger voters and African Americans who never were interested in voting during elections before. Hillary had also attracted more women and Latino voters more than ever before. In polls after polls against John McCain, Obama and Hillary were ahead of McCain by a single digit.

But, it takes 2 of them to combine their equally strong forces to be practically unbeatable.

A Barack Obama-Hillary Clinton Democratic presidential ticket would combine their respective leads into double digits. Obama won in Western and Southern states (except Arkansas that went to Hillary) while Hillary won in bigger northeastern states, and California, and the battleground states of Ohio, Pennsylvania, and Florida. A combination of both Obama and Hillary in one Democratic presidential ticket would make it formidable.

Lyrical Illustrations Seven:

Lyric #33 titled *WE'RE 2 OF A KIND* is a duet of both Barack Obama & Michelle, as well as of Hillary Clinton & Bill. Because Obama and Hillary have partners with which they are respectively paired to be considered positively "2 of a kind," so when they run together as a presidential and a vice-presidential team, they are equally highly regarded crossover "2 of a kind."

Just to give 2 examples: (1) Obama & Michelle are 2 of a kind, for they both graduated from Harvard Law School, while Hillary & Bill also graduated from Yale Law School, each of which had contributed 7 & 5 of presidents in American history. (2) If we combine the 2 with Obama & Hillary Harvard & Yale respectively, that would be 12 U.S. presidents, the biggest group of sources of U.S. presidents!

Obama would increase the share of Harvard to 8 U.S. presidents. Interestingly, the last time a *full* Harvard graduate won the U.S. presidency was when Sen. John F. Kennedy won it in 1960. (The incumbent George W. Bush is both a graduate of Harvard & Yale, so he is only ½ Harvardian & ½ Eli). On the other hand, Yale graduates won 4 U.S. presidencies out of 6 since Gerald Ford in 1976, followed by George Bush, Sr., Bill Clinton, until the incumbent George W. Bush.

33. WE'RE 2 OF A KIND (Obama & Michelle's & Hillary & Bill's respective duets)

SHE:	(1) We both believe in lifelong love, Faithful through ups and downs of life
HE:	Till we leave for heaven above, We'll always be husband and wife.
TWO:	We're truly two of a kind. We're surely of the same mind. Without life, we can't be loving Without love, we can't be living. When we slight friendship, we speed failing. When we stop dreaming, we start dying.
SHE:	(2) We both depend on faithful friends To be with us when we're joyful
HE:	More so with us when we're in pains. Because of them we're successful.
TWO:	We're truly two of a kind. We're surely of the same mind.

Without life, we can't be loving
Without love, we can't be living.
When we slight friendship, we speed
failing.
When we stop dreaming, we start dying.

SHE: (3) We both hanker for daring dreams:
US children grow up happy.

HE: And all the world's children, like them,
Will be just as happy as they

TWO: We're truly two of a kind.
We're surely of the same mind.
Without life, we can't be loving.
Without love, we can't be living.
When we slight friendship, we speed
failing.
When we stop dreaming, we start dying.

Lyric #34 titled *LIKE THE MOON OVER SAN FRANCISCO* is dedicated to Gabriella Tamburrini of Rome, Italy, a former student of author Benjamin at the Newark Adult School, Newark, CA. Before Theresa went to heaven, she asked Benjamin if he had someone in person in mind to take her place; if so she wanted to meet her so she could approve of her. Benjamin invited Gabriella, thinking that she was single, but then she asked, "Can I bring my husband, too?"

She and her husband, Mario, had dinner with Benjamin & Theresa's home in Fremont, CA. Theresa said, "Benjie, she is really good." "But, she belongs to someone already," Benjamin replied. That was when Theresa said, "I have a back up plan. Just ask Irene for my diary when I'm gone. I've explained everything there." Exactly 25 days after that conversation, Theresa went to heaven on July 10, 2002 when she was only 67 years old (she had an incurable heart disease).

LIKE THE MOON OVER SAN FRANCISCO was commissioned by Gabriella, in front of her husband, after Benjamin had written 7 other previous songs thinking she was single. To this day, Gabriella and her husband remain Benjamin's forever friends, and they have an open invitation for him to live in their house in Rome, whether they are home or not.

34. LIKE THE MOON OVER SAN FRANCISCO
(to Gabriella Tamburrini)

(1) Just as you graciously ordered:
  "Write a song with the moon in it."
I'll do, as one quite surrendered,
  Whatever whenever you wish it
Like the moon over San Francisco
  I've no light to show my radiance.
I'm fully satisfied to glow
  Just reflecting your sun's brilliance
As your sun is always with you
  He will light your life everyday.
I promise to be there with you
  During the night when you need me

(2) I've warmed you at the Golden Gate,
  Fisherman's Wharf, and marina,
In the "Don Quijote Ballet"
  At the War Memorial Opera
Like the moon over San Francisco
  I've no light to show my radiance.
I'm fully satisfied to glow
  Just reflecting your sun's brilliance
As your sun is always with you
  He will light your life everyday.
I promise to be there with you
  During the night when you need me

(3) And when you get back to Roma
  I may seem too far, far away.
Think of me at the Opera
  When once you were so close to me
Like the moon over San Francisco
  I've no light to show my radiance.
I'm fully satisfied to glow
  Just reflecting your sun's brilliance
As your sun is always with you
  He will light your life everyday.
I promise to be there with you
  During the night when you need me

Lyric #35 titled *ALOHA LOE,* a hula, was especially written for 3 sisters whose first names formed the word LOE (Lyza, Onel, & Elisha Feliciano) who performed the hula dance at one of the SACSDAPFRI (Society of Asian Cultural & Social Dancers for Physical Fitness, Inc.) at the Centerville Park Community Center in Fremont, CA. The tune of the song is the original tune of *ALOHA OE* composed by the last Queen Lilioukalini of Hawaii.

35. ALOHA LOE (performed by Lyza, Onel, & Elisha Feliciano; tune: "Aloha Oe")

(1) Proudly, we bring you this dance of Hawaii,
Islands of the western blue Pacific sea
    With hips shaking down here and hands waving up there
    We dance this Aloha LOE anywhere.
Aloha LOE, aloha LOE
We're Feliciano sisters, one, two, and three:
    First, Lyza; next, Onel, and then, Elisha.
    We're "Hug Ur Love Aloha."

(2) Some have said that in a million years Hawaii
Will sink to the bottom of the deep blue sea
    But no one among us can live that many years.
    We might as well enjoy every moment, dears.
    Aloha LOE, aloha LOE
We're Feliciano sisters, one, two, and three:
    First, Lyza; next, Onel, and then, Elisha.
We're "Hug Ur Love Aloha."

(3) Nor can we just keep on dancing without an end.
While we're young, we take this chance to entertain.
    So, the sweet memories of our get-together
    Will remain with us forever and ever!
    Aloha LOE, aloha LOE
We're Feliciano sisters, one, two, and three:
    First, Lyza; next, Onel, and then, Elisha.
We're "Hug Ur Love Aloha."

Lyric #36 titled *SACSDAPFRI THEME SONG,* a cha-cha, is dedicated to President David M. Tamayo of SACSDAPFRI (Society of Asian Social & Cultural Dancers for Physical Fitness & Recreation, Inc.), with 2nd Veep "Louie" Garcia, Secretary Remy Miranda Pineda and dance instructor Nancy

Estefenel. This association meets every Sunday from 4:30 to 8:30 p.m. for its weekly dance. Author Benjamin has served as SACSDAPFRI Chaplain from its start in 2006.

36. SACSDAPFRI THEME SONG (to David Tamayo, President; tune: cha-cha)

(Nancy Estefenel & Inquirers)

(1) We all know exercise promotes health, cha-cha-cha
There's no doubt it even prolongs life
But, I find it hard to exercise
Believe me, my reasons are a lot
Thirty minutes daily is too much
It isn't interesting enough
It's no fun doing it by myself
I have many things to do besides, cha-cha-cha

(2) On Monday, I feel blue and sickly, cha-cha-cha
On Tuesday, I always keep busy
On Wednesday, I shop for grocery
On Thursday, I attend PTA
On Friday, I date with my buddy
On Saturday, I care for family
On Sunday, I sleep tired and lonely
I've no time for more activity, cha-cha-cha

("Loiue" Garcia, Remy Miranda Pineda & Members)

(3) Sunday afternoon's for SACSDAPFRI,
    cha-cha-cha
You have no more excuses really
Feed your spirit, and mind, and body
You will be in church very early
The rest of the day, you're fully free
Everyone around you is friendly
You can have fun and still be healthy
Dance every Sunday at SACSDAPFRI, cha-cha-cha

(4) On Monday, you wake up quite happy,
    cha-cha-cha
On Tuesday, you do work snappily
On Wednesday, you buy foods variedly
On Thursday, you lead at PTA

On Friday, you excite your buddy
On Saturday, all care for family
On Sunday, you can sleep restfully
When you dance weekly at SACSDAPFRI,
    cha-cha-cha

Lyric #37 titled *NEW "ANNIVERSARY WALTZ"* as it says is a waltz, dedicated to Malou Flores, Treasurer of SACSDAPFRI by her husband, SACSFDAPFRI executive vice-president Frank Flores, and also to co-author Patricia II by Benjamin. Sing to the traditional tune of Al Dubin & Jimmy McHugh's *ANNIVERSARY WALTZ*.

37. NEW "ANNIVERSARY WALTZ"
(To Malou Flores; Patricia II, etc.; tune: traditional)

(1) Oh, I remember the day we were wed
    Through all the years and places that had gone by.
I can't believe that you, so special indeed,
    Would have married a man as humble as I
    Dear, as I looked at you very closely,
    I heard angels singing songs to your beauty.
    I sensed my heart feeling more than words can say:
    "Heaven united you and me!"

(2) Were I to review the course of our life
    To see if there is a need for any change
In one or both of us as husband and wife,
    We'll only wish to live the same way again!
    Dear, as I looked at you very closely,
    I heard angels singing songs to your beauty.
    I sensed my heart feeling more than words can say:
    "Heaven united you and me!"

(3) So, on this day of days, we celebrate
    The many wonderful joys of life we share.
Although we have grown with a few wrinkles, yet
    Our love has remained ever true forever!
    Dear, as I looked at you very closely,
    I heard angels singing songs to your beauty.
    I sensed my heart feeling more than words can say:
    "Heaven united you and me!"

8

Faithful Friendships Are Win-Win Situations

Many people make friends for what they think they can get out of the relationship. Such people often do not have lasting friendships. Because as soon as the one being taken advantage of realizes what is happening, s/he more likely than not, terminates the relationship.

A more lasting friendship is that made "without any strings attached." In other words, friendship is for friendship's sake.

The most lasting friendships of all, however, are those made for the sake of the friend. This is the kind that leads to a win-win situation, in which both friends end up enjoying the relationship, and cooperate with each other to enhance even what they already have. Such a friendship may even be considered "as more than love." Jesus described this type of friendship as heroic: "Greater love has no man (or woman) than this that he is willing to lay down his life for the sake of his friend(s)" (*see* definition of a hero in Chapter 2 above).

Lyrical Illustrations Eight;

Lyric #38 titled *WE ALWAYS PLAY TO WIN* describes the type of friendship that exists in the best of lifelong marriages. Both Barack Obama and Michelle, and Hillary Clinton & Bill have that kind of relationship, and this lyric is dedicated to both couples. Both Barack Obama and Bill Clinton had expressed more than once that any criticism of their respective spouses, should be directed to them.

Theresa also felt that way about her lifelong marriage to author Benjamin, so that just a couple of weeks before she went to heaven in 2002, she told him: "Please get married again, so that you can make some other woman as happy as you have made me for more than 40 years."

38. WE ALWAYS PLAY TO WIN (Obama & Michelle, & Hillary & Bill duet)

SHE: Love is a game you choose.
                  It's not whether you win
            And/or whether you lose
                  It's how you play the game!

                                                    (Echo:)
HE: The game of love we choose   (**SHE:** The game we choose.
                  Brings to us peace or pain.   Brings peace or pain
            We do not play to lose.   Not play to lose.
                  We only play to win   Just play to win.)

HE: Love is a game you choose.
                  It's not whether you win
            And/or whether you lose
                  It's how you play the game!

TWO: The game of love we choose
                  Brings to us grace and gain.
            We never play to lose.
                  We always play to win!

Lyric #39 titled *WE'RE 2 OF A KIND, ARNIE* is dedicated to Gov. Arnold Schwarzenegger (*R, CA*) which shows the comparison and contrast between his career and author Benjamin. There is one major negative similarity between them in that being both foreign-born "they cannot be president of the USA." Nevertheless they "can serve our country some other way."

39. WE'RE 2 OF A KIND, ARNIE (to Governor Arnold Schwarzenneger {R, CA})

(1) We both know marriage is for life
We searched everywhere for a wife
    In the U.S., you found Maria
    In Myanmar, I found Theresa
We're two of a kind, Arnie,
Both born outside this country
    You're Austrian-American, and
    I'm Philippine-American.
U.S. president, we cannot be
But, we can still serve another way.

(2) You were a Hollywood actor
I was a college professor
    Both involved a lot of actions
    These 2 of noblest professions
We're two of a kind, Arnie,
Both born outside this country
    You're Austrian-American, and
    I'm Philippine-American.
U.S. president, we cannot be
But, we can still serve another way.

(3) You're California's governor
That's like a president's honor
    Dianne Feinstein, our senator
    Made me personal counselor
We're two of a kind, Arnie,
Both born outside this country
    You're Austrian-American, and
    I'm Philippine-American.
U.S. president, we cannot be
But, we can still serve another way.

(4) Orrin Hatch may also succeed
To have the constitution changed
    Then, be president, do you mind?
    If you do, I'm not far behind!
We're two of a kind, Arnie,

Both born outside this country
You're Austrian-American, and
I'm Philippine-American.
U.S. president, we cannot be
But, we can still serve another way.

Lyric #40 titled *DON'T BUILD A FENCE ALONG THE RIO GRANDE* is dedicated to U.S. president Ronald Reagan, another Republican, because he established the pattern that fences are not effective to keep people in or out of a country. In the same way that he demanded that the "Berlin wall be torn down," so do we think that if he were alive today, he would be opposed to erecting another physical wall at the Rio Grande.

40. DON'T BUILD A FENCE ALONG THE RIO GRANDE (to President Ronald Reagan)

(1) You can't build a fence to keep people in
That we learned in the city of Berlin.
It took U.S. Ronald Reagan to call
"Mister Gorbachev, please tear down this wall!"
Don't build a fence along the Rio Grande
Let it be free like at the St. Lawrence.
Don't build a fence along the Rio Grande.
You can't stop southern dreamers from coming.
Here in America they have a chance
To work, to love, and to go on living
South of the Rio Grande, they have no chance
And no hope, but to be slowly dying

(2) You can't build a fence to keep people out
If it's greener this side, they'll soon find out.
Then, who will call to tear down Rio Grande's wall?
Fidel Castro, or his brother Raul?
Don't build a fence along the Rio Grande
Let it be free like at the St. Lawrence
Don't build a fence along the Rio Grande.
You can't stop southern dreamers from coming.
Here in America they have a chance
To work, to love, and to go on living
South of the Rio Grande, they have no chance
And no hope, but to be slowly dying

(3) You can't build a fence to cover the sky
If people can't come by land, they'll by sea,
Or, like birds with wings, they can even fly
For a chance to work, to love, and live free.
Don't build a fence along the Rio Grande
    Let it be free like at the St. Lawrence
Don't build a fence along the Rio Grande.
    You can't stop southern dreamers from coming.
Here in America they have a chance
    To work, to love, and to go on living
South of the Rio Grande, they have no chance
    And no hope, but to be slowly dying

Lyric #41 *"ALL THE WORLD'S A STAGE,"* a school theme song, dedicated to Charlie McCrystle, head of the Newark Adult School, Newark, CA, who hired author Benjamin to teach English in 1989. When the latter objected because his teaching credential was in Math from Mills (Women's) College, Oakland, CA, Mr. McCrystle said that Benjamin could continue teaching in his school, provided the latter would take a subject or 2 towards his ESL teaching credential every summer from the California State University in San Jose, CA. As soon as he received his ESL teaching credential, Benjamin was given the Adult ESL Teacher of the Year Award in 2000-2001 by the Newark Unified School District, Newark, CA.

41. ALL THE WORLD'S A STAGE"
(to Charlie McCrystle; lyric based on Shakespeare)

"All the world's a stage; [all the world's a stage]…"
We've come from North or South America,
Or Europe, or Asia, or Africa
Today we meet in Newark, California.

(1) "…Men and women are merely players…"
You're all very pleasant women.   (We're)
And we're all agreeable men.   (And you're)
We've a grand design from heaven.
    "All the world's a stage; [all the world's a stage]…"
    We've come from North or South America,
    Or Europe, or Asia, or Africa
    Today we meet in Newark, California.

(2) "They have their exits and ... entrances..."
Our entrances weren't long ago.
Our exits, as far as we know,
May be a whole life-time to go
    "All the world's a stage; [all the world's a stage]…"
    We've come from North or South America,
    Or Europe, or Asia, or Africa
    Today we meet in Newark, California.

(3) "...One man in his time plays many parts...."
We've played very different parts.
We're always ready in our hearts
When our peaceful world-conquest starts
    "All the world's a stage; [all the world's a stage]…"
    We've come from North or South America,
    Or Europe, or Asia, or Africa
    Today we meet in Newark, California.

Lyric #42 titled *FOR, I CARE FOR YOU* is dedicated to co-author Patricia II by Benjamin. Because she does not allow him to say "I love you," the alternative is "I care for you." The former can lead to marriage, the latter does not. But, the degree of concern is not any less.

42. FOR, I CARE FOR YOU (to Patricia II)

(1) You don't want me to ever say,
    Your Dad doesn't say them even:
"I love you" now or any day.
    I do care enough to listen.
I'll say what you want me to say.
    I'll do what you want me to do.
I'll be what you want me to be.
    For, I care for you.
(2) You don't want me to try to hold
    You, until you're ready for it.
That may take a long time all told.
    I care to do nothing but wait.
I'll say what you want me to say.
    I'll do what you want me to do.
I'll be what you want me to be.
    For, I care for you.

(3) You don't want me to ever be
    A rude, inconsiderate man
To you or another lady
    I care to be part of your plan.
I'll say what you want me to say.
    I'll do what you want me to do.
I'll be what you want me to be.
    For, I care for you.

It was no accident that Martin Luther King, Jr., who was a Baptist preacher in Atlanta, GA, also gave the most memorable message of the civil rights movement delivered in front of the Lincoln Memorial in Washington, DC, titled *I HAVE A DREAM* on August 28, 1963. There are 2 types of dreamers: secular and religious. There is no doubt that Martin Luther King, Jr. was not a secular dreamer. He was a religious Christian deathless dreamer.

To author Benjamin, it does not seem that long ago when he became part of the Yale delegation led by one of the greatest Ivy-League civil rights activists of the time, the Reverend Chaplain William Sloane Coffin of the University Chapel, that park themselves not too far away from the center of the crowd of thousands to listen to Dr. Martin Luther King, Jr. that hot, late August day in front of the Lincoln Memorial, Washington DC.

It is a matter of divine opportunity for Barack Obama, who recognizes that he is one of the most blessed, not to say, luckiest recipients of the legacy of Dr. King, to coincide his epoch-making acceptance speech as presidential standard bearer at the Democratic Party convention in Denver, CO with the 45th anniversary of the *I HAVE A DREAM* message on August 28, 2008!

PART III

Diehard Dreamers' Dreams Don't Die

(Civil rights leader Martin Luther King,
Jr. & his wife, Coretta Scott King)

"I have a dream that someday my own Black children will walk hand in hand with White children ... on the way to the Promised Land." (Martin Luther King, Jr.)

9

Dreamers Are Born-Again &
Timothy-Type

Religious deathless dreamers are of 2 types, as there are only 2 ways to become a Christian, according to the Bible: (1) being born-again as in the case of Barack Obama, and (2) being reared in a Christian household as in the case of Hillary. There are some conservative evangelical Christians who consider being born-again as the sole criterion for being a Christian, so therefore would question the genuineness of Hillary's Methodist Christian faith.

Author Benjamin has surprising news for his fellow-Christian evangelical brethren. Benjamin was born-again at the age of 15 through the ministry of Rev. Patricio Albano, a Christian and Missionary Alliance Evangelical Church, in Zamboanga, the Southern Philippines where he was born. Benjamin was a North American missionary professor *Emeritus* to the Evangelical Theological Seminary (ETSI), in Yogyakarta, and former Dean of the Asian Theological (Evangelica) Seminary in Manila, Philippines in the early 1980's.

Benjamin's surprising news is: except for the present George W. Bush, Jimmy Carter, and possibly Ronald Reagan, who were born-again believers, all the 40 other U.S. presidents – 39 Protestant and 1 Catholic (John F. Kennedy) were mainline religious Christians like Hillary.

Some fellow-evangelical Christians are not satisfied in questioning Hillary's Christian faith; they would even question the born-again Christian faith of Barack Obama! They are skeptical that Obama is a Christian deathless dreamer. Some would admit that he might be a religious dreamer, but not of the Christian, but rather of the Muslim faith.

Benjamin has another surprising news for his fellow-evangelical Christians: (a) Obama was led to the Jesus as His personal Lord and Savior by Rev. Jeremiah Wright, (b) who also baptized him as a follow-up of his profession of faith, (c) officiated at his wedding with his wife Michelle Robinson-Obama, and (d) baptized his 2 children.

If Rev. Jeremiah Wright was instrumental in leading Obama to Jesus as His Personal Lord and Savior, why did Obama disown him as his pastor? Obama disowned Wright for certain claims of the latter that he did not agree with. But, that neither invalidates the latter's role in leading him to Jesus, nor his role in leading Michelle Robinson, Oprah Winfrey, and the thousands of other Christian born-again believers, both Black and White, who regularly worship at the Trinity United Church, Chicago, IL today.

Lyrical Illustration Nine:

Lyric #43 titled *WE'RE "ALL THINGS TO ALL MEN* (& WOMEN) has as its basis the writings of Paul in the New Teatament. It is updated and applied to the similarities and differences in the careers of Sen. Barack Obama and author Benjamin. For the similarities between Obama and Benjamin: (a) they were both born on islands in the Pacific Ocean, (b) they spent sometime in the biggest Muslim country in the world, Indonesia; (c) they graduated in Ivy-League universities, Obama in Harvard (Law School) & Benjamin in Yale (Divinity School), and (d) they are both born-again believers. The last similarity is most important!

The differences were even more marked: in every step, Obama was destined to be considered for the presidency of the United States, like John F. Kennedy, Abraham Lincoln, or George Washington as he was born in a state of the United States of America, Hawaii, but Benjamin was not.

43. WE'RE "ALL THINGS TO ALL MEN"
(& WOMEN) (to Obama by Benjamin)

We were born amid the sea
You, in near Hawaii
I, in the far Philippines
But, there is a difference:
Hawaii is American
Philippines is foreign land
You can run for president
I can be a citizen
We lived in Indonesia

You, in modern Jakarta
I, in Yogya, so ancient
But, there is a difference:
You had secular studies
In your public school classes
I served as missionary
In a church seminary

We were both Ivy-Leaguers
You, a Harvard Law scholar
I, a Yale Missions student
But, there is a difference:
You work in public service
Informed by Christian witness
I teach ways of a Christian
To any public servant

We're born-again believers
You, led by Wright, your mentor,
Albano led me, a teen,
But, there is a difference:
You disliked Wright's extreme views
But, through him you found Jesus
My mentor lacked prominence;
I'm saved by his persistence.

Lyric #44 titled *CHRISTIAN WOMAN, YOU'RE EVERYTHING* is dedicated to Hillary who was reared by her parents as a God-fearing Christian lady, especially through her attendance at her Mom Dorothy Emma Howell-Rodham's Sunday School class in the Methodist Church in Parkridge, IL. During her teen years, Rev. Don Jones, a youth pastor started his ministry in her home church, and it was he as her early mentor who led her to a deeper commitment to Jesus Christ especially in the area of Christian social service.

As the lyric summarizes Hillary's Christian character, it is that (a) of a forgiven sinner, (b) a never complaining God's servant, and (c) "a saint who will be crowned a queen!" With Hillary as a model, the ladies among our Readers can become exemplary Christians as well.

44. CHRISTIAN WOMAN, YOU'RE EVERYTHING
(Dedicated to Hillary Clinton)

Christian woman, you're everything.
    You're a sinner, but forgiven.
You're a servant, never complaining.
    You're a saint, who'll be crowned a queen.

(1) It's not where you have come so far
    It's where so far you have now come.
It's not important what you are
    It's crucial who you have become.
It's following Christ no matter
    What obstacles you'll overcome.
Christian woman, you're everything.
    You're a sinner, but forgiven.
You're a servant, never complaining.
    You're a saint, who'll be crowned a queen.

(2) It's not regretting what might have been
    Thank God for your sure salvation.
It's not fretting how hard the moment
    Trust His Spirit for direction.
It's looking forward to heaven
    When you have finished your mission
Christian woman, you're everything.
    You're a sinner, but forgiven.
You're a servant, never complaining.
    You're a saint, who'll be crowned a queen.

(3) It's not digging past history
    To see what's worth remembering.
It's not doing activity
    Even though it's quite exciting
It's all living to get ready
    For your coming heavenly King!
Christian woman, you're everything.
    You're a sinner, but forgiven.
You're a servant, never complaining.
    You're a saint, who'll be crowned a queen.

Lyric #45 titled *BEFORE ANN DUNHAM WENT TO HEAVEN* is dedicated to Obama's Mom. The real issue that might be controversial in the life of Ann Dunham is the fact of our certainty that she is waiting up in heaven for her children and grandchildren. Dr. Billy Graham has an answer to this matter of certainty of salvation which is that "on this side of heaven, we are not to be dogmatic as to who is saved or not saved. Only God decides whom He brings to Jesus our Savior."

The authors of this book believe in a just and a loving God. For the benefit of all humankind, in her own pioneering way, Ann Dunham was the means of unity of our Christian faith with the rest of peace-loving religions of the world including Judaism, Mormonism, Hinduism, Sikhism, Buddhism, Shintoism, Taoism, Bahaism, Animism, Muhammedanism, and Atheism.

And for the sake of America, she was also in a very personal way God's instrument in moving forward the assimilation of all divergent races into one American people (*E pluribus, unum*) through her children: African American Barack Obama, Jr. and Asian (Indonesian) American Maya Soetero-Ng.

The uniqueness of Ann Dunham was not only in the way she lived, but also in the way she died. She was the first (Theresa, author Benjamin's Burmese wife was only the second) person ever who decreed that her ashes be strewn in the Pacific Ocean, so that she could be connected all at once through its water with Kenya and Indonesia, homelands of both her husbands: Barack Obama, Sr. and Lolo Soetero respectively.

45. BEFORE ANN DUNHAM WENT TO HEAVEN
(to Obama's Mom from Kansas)

The continents of the earth divide us
But, the oceans around them unite us.
In life, we meet people in many places.
Although we were born in separate countries,
We may make our earthly home in between
But, our final home is waiting in heaven

(1) Ann Dunham said before going to heaven:
"Don't bury me in Kansas where I was born.
Just drop my ashes in Aloha's ocean
It's like being buried with my first husband
For the water that touches my Aloha
Is the same water that touches his Kenya"
The continents of the earth divide us

But, the oceans around them unite us.
In life, we meet people in many places.
Although we were born in separate countries,
We may make our earthly home in between
But, our final home is waiting in heaven

(2) Ann Dunham said before going to heaven:
"Don't bury me in Kansas where I was born.
Just drop my ashes in Aloha's ocean
It's like being buried with my next husband
For the water that touches my Aloha
Is the same water that touches Indonesia."
The continents of the earth divide us
But, the oceans around them unite us.
In life, we meet people in many places.
Although we were born in separate countries,
We may make our earthly home in between
But, our final home is waiting in heaven

(3) When it was time for Ann to go to heaven
They didn't bury her body where she was born
They spread her ashes in Aloha's ocean
'Twas like being buried with her two husbands
For the water that touches her Aloha
Also touches Kenya and Indonesia.
The continents of the earth divide us
But, the oceans around them unite us.
In life, we meet people in many places.
Although we were born in separate countries,
We may make our earthly home in between
But, our final home is waiting in heaven.

Lyric #46 is titled *IF YOU BELIEVE* dedicated to the Christian and Missionary Alliance pastor who led author Benjamin to Jesus Christ at the age of 15, the Rev. Patricio Albano in the Southern Philippines. The message of *IF YOU BELIEVE* may be summarized by the word OBEY (O is for obey; B is for believe; E is for Educate, & Y is for Yes). All 12 disciples, except 1, Judas, were of the OBEY-type followers of Jesus! Do you count yourself an OBEY?

46. IF YOU BELIEVE (Dedicated to Rev. Patricio Albano; Text: John 14:6)

Jesus Christ says, "I am the Way.
I am the Truth that sets you free.
I am the Life no one has lived.
Just follow Me, and you'll believe."

(1) Jesus is the Way to heaven.
     He is the Truth that frees all slaves.
He is the Life that has no end.
     These you can have, if you believe.
Jesus Christ says, "I am the Way.
I am the Truth that sets you free.
I am the Life no one has lived.
Just follow Me, and you'll believe."

(2) Ask Him and you will be given.
     Give and in turn you will receive.
Knock and the door will be open.
     These you can do, if you believe.
Jesus Christ says, "I am the Way.
I am the Truth that sets you free.
I am the Life no one has lived.
Just follow Me, and you'll believe."

(3) He'll teach you as dearest dreamer.
     He'll transform you ever so brave.
He'll turn you the greatest lover.
     These you can be, if you believe.
Jesus Christ says, "I am the Way.
I am the Truth that sets you free.
I am the Life no one has lived.
Just follow Me, and you'll believe."

Lyric #47 titled *O TAKE ME TO PHILADELPHIA* is author Benjamin's biographical song in which he reveals that he had never gone to Philadelphia, the playground of Franklin, because he did not feel worthy to present himself there, "a hallow ground."

For fear that he might never be "worthy enough" to go to the "city-of-brotherly-love" on his own, he writes this lyric, requesting that he might be taken to Philadelphia "ere he goes to heaven."

The lyric reveals that author Benjamin was named after Benjamin Franklin of Philadelphia, but did not say who made the decision to do so. They were no other than Lucas Camins, Sr., and Crispina Lazo-Camins (later Ferrari), Benjamin's parents. They would have named their first-born son after George Washington, whom they thought was "the greatest American," but they thought that their son being foreign-born, he would never become U.S. president, so they settled on naming their son after Benjamin Franklin whom they considered the second greatest American instead.

Fast forward to the start of the 21st century: the well-known historian, W.H. Brands of Texas A. & M. University, publishes a definitive biography of Benjamin Franklin, with the title *THE FIRST AMERICAN*. On page 8 of his book, Brands writes that Franklin was "the first American because he was the first Englishman who realized he had a different nationality, and he was also the first American in terms of greatness, for the reason that while George Washington commanded the U.S. troops that defeated the British decisively in the battle of Yorktown, it was Franklin who raised the money to feed and equip the American soldiers!"

47. O TAKE ME TO PHILADELPHIA
(Tune: Don't Go to Far Zamboanga")

(1) Don't you know, don't you know, I've only one dream
   That I've wished to fulfill since I was a teen?
Don't you know, don't you know, I got Franklin's name
   But, his Philadelphia home I haven't seen?
   O take me to Philadelphia,
      O take me, ere I go to heaven,
   O take me, with my Patricia
      To see the old playground of Franklin

(2) Don't you know, don't you know, that I lived so near
   The city-of-brotherly-love's "holy ground?"
Don't you know, don't you know, I didn't go sooner
   But waited all my life to be Philly-bound?
   O take me to Philadelphia,
      O take me, ere I go to heaven,
   O take me, with my Patricia
      To see the old playground of Franklin

(3) Don't you know, don't you know, I'm getting too old
    Almost as old as Senator John McCain?
Don't you, don't you know, Franklin's life has told
    We can serve well without being president?
    O take me to Philadelphia,
       O take me, ere I go to heaven,
    O take me, with my Patricia
       To see the old playground of Franklin

.

10

What It Takes To Change America

To change America requires involvement on the part of individual Americans, like you, our Readers. To be able to do so requires only one major qualification, a quality education. There is no substitute for an excellent education. In some other countries of the world, sometimes "it is not what you know but whom you know" that is more important in getting you a job. There is too much nepotism.

In America, you must have the necessary educational degree to qualify for a job. Along with your diploma, you must also know what you are supposed to have studied. Some practical aspects of your job, you can learn by experience.

A high school diploma in our modern technological world is no longer enough. There is too much competition from other countries whose best educational leaders might have studied in the best American universities. Even a 2-year college degree may barely be sufficient, unless of course, if you do not aspire higher than the lowest paying and most menial of jobs.

A college degree or better yet, a master's degree in your field, and technical knowledge related to your job are absolutely necessary. Reading newspapers and even watching television are no longer enough to keep you updated on the latest information that are necessary for success in your work. Whatever your job is, knowledge in the use of the Internet is a must.

If you are motivated, aspire to finish the doctoral level of your profession. Do not ever think that you cannot afford to get the highest education that you are interested in and have a talent for. To obtain the highest possible education in America is "never a money problem." It is a matter of having "the best idea." If you are academically inclined, get a Ph.D. in any field. Try to get a Ph.D. degree from any reputable university, including an Ivy-League one. When you do, you can be an expert not only in your own special field, but also in several other fields.

Lyrical Illustrations Ten:

Lyric #48 is titled *OBAMA'S ADVICE TO WESLEYAN UNIVERSITY STUDENTS*. This lyric is mainly based on the Commencement address which Obama gave to the 2008 graduating class of Wesleyan University, Middletown, CT, in lieu of his colleague, Sen. Ted Kennedy (*D, MA*) who could not make it because he was diagnosed with cancer. Author Benjamin does not expect Ted Kennedy to remember this, since his positive attitude to others is proverbial extending to loved ones, his colleagues across all political spectrum, old and new friends, and even perfect strangers. One of those strangers was Benjamin who just happened to visit the U.S. Senate after the assassination of his brother, President John F. Kennedy, to express a "belated condolence." As everyone knows although Kennedys in private and public service abound, Benjamin shook the hands of only one, Ted Kennedy's!

Obama's advice to consider public service as one's life calling can also apply to any of our Readers, both male and female.

48. OBAMA'S ADVICE TO WESLEYAN UNIVERSITY STUDENTS (of Middletown, CT)

I care to cover for Ted Kennedy
　　To charge you with a two-fold commission:
To choose to change the course of our country
　　And to cherish one man's contribution

(1) I commend you, my fellow-Americans,
This year's graduating seniors at Wesleyan　　　　(i.e. 2008)
　　That when you leave this great university
　　Try to work in the service of your country.
It is a privilege to be an American
Even much more so as a graduate of Wesleyan
　　Everyone in the world has an American dream
　　But, some of us have found it impossible to dream

(2) I commend you, my fellow-Americans,
This year's graduating seniors at Wesleyan
    That when you leave this great university
    Try to work in the service of your country
You and I have had helpful parents, friends, and mentors
Who taught us, changed our lives, and remain our counselors
    They have not thought of being given any reward
    But, gratitude for their deed and "to pass it forward"

(3) I commend you, my fellow-Americans,
This year's graduating seniors at Wesleyan
    That when you leave this great university
    Try to work in the service of your country
You can serve your country for your own satisfaction
You're not required to serve by a law of our nation
    Service has always been part of our country's story
    Be that one person to extend our great history

Lyric #49 is titled *HILLARY'S ADVICE TO STUDENTS* of Wellesley Women's College, which can apply to any of our women Readers. Hillary herself had repeated many times during the presidential primary campaign season of 2007-2008 that in public service from the humblest to the highest office of U.S. presidency, "sometimes the best man for the job is a woman." Do you agree?

49. HILLARY'S ADVICE TO STUDENTS
(of Wellesley Women's College, Wellesley, MA)

(1) These were my thoughts when I came to Wellesley:
"I'll try to be the best in my study,
    But, because I am only a woman
    My life's purpose is 'to stand by my man.'
When God sends the right man to marry me
I'll help him to be the best he can be."
    But, God led me to serve differently:
    "Sometimes the best man for the job is me!"

(2) Here is my advice to you at Wellesley:
"Do try to be the best in your study
    Don't ever say you're only a woman
    Whose life's purpose is to 'stand by your man'
When God sends you to marry the right man
You'll help him to be the best as you can.
    But, He might give you another work, too:
    'Sometimes the best man for the job is you.'"

(3) Someday, when you have your own family,
With as many children who are happy,
    Tell your sons: "The world was made for a man
    But, you might need the help of a woman
If you turn out to be very lucky
To marry one with talent and beauty
    God might ask you: help your wife in His plan:
    '... [When] the best man for the job is a woman'"

(4) Persuade your daughters to come to Wellesley
They'll learn not just academic study
    Tell them: "Though the world was made for a man
    'Behind each great man is a great woman.'
If you turn out to be very lucky
To be picked by a good man to marry
    When God gives you a task he'll understand:
    '... [That] the best man for the job is a woman'"

Lyric #50 titled *CATHERINE'S HARVARD DREAM SONG* is dedicated to Benjamin's Vietnamese American teenage co-author in early 2008, of *HILLARY IS THE BEST CHOICE,* Catherine Lien who is in her sophomore year at Washington High School, Fremont, CA.

Catherine is a girl of many talents, like her mentor, author Benjamin, and she could be (a) a future writer. She thought of studying either at Columbia University to be (b) a teacher, or at MIT to be (c) an engineer, or even at Yale to be (d) a lawyer like Hillary and Bill Clinton.

However, her real dream is to be a doctor of medicine someday, and for that "the best place for her study" is no less than Barack and Michelle Obama's Alma Mater, Harvard University.

50. CATHERINE'S HARVARD DREAM SONG
(Dedicated to Catherine Lien)

If I want to be a teacher,
　　Columbia is the place to be.
If I want to be engineer,
　　I'll have to go to M.I.T.
If I want to be a lawyer,
　　It'll be Yale University.
But, I want to be a doctor,
　　Harvard is the best place for me!

(1) I need to work hard and study
With a plan to follow strictly
I'll share responsibility
So, my roommates will be happy.
If I want to be a teacher,
　　Columbia is the place to be.
If I want to be engineer,
　　I'll have to go to M.I.T.
If I want to be a lawyer,
　　It'll be Yale University.
But, I want to be a doctor,
　　Harvard is the best place for me!

(2) I must become strong and healthy.
I'll exercise regularly.
And when there's opportunity,
I'll try to walk a bit each day.
If I want to be a teacher,
　　Columbia is the place to be.
If I want to be engineer,
　　I'll have to go to M.I.T.
If I want to be a lawyer,
　　It'll be Yale University.
But, I want to be a doctor,
　　Harvard is the best place for me!

(3) I have to grow spiritually.
I'll go to church every Sunday.
I'll be closer to God, I pray,
And read His Word to guide my way.
If I want to be a teacher,
    Columbia is the place to be.
If I want to be engineer,
    I'll have to go to M.I.T.
If I want to be a lawyer,
    It'll be Yale University.
But, I want to be a doctor,
    Harvard is the best place for me!

Lyric #51 titled *SHAWN, YOU DESERVE A YALE DREAM* is dedicated to Shawn Young of Chicago, IL, hometown of Barack & Michelle Robinson-Obama, birthplace of Hillary Rodham-Clinton, and of course, Oprah Winfrey. According to the *Readers' Digest* issue of August, 2005, Shawn Young will be among the 14 most influential Americans in the future.

When author Benjamin found out that from the list of the faculty of Greenville College, Chicago where he teaches Contemporary Lyrics, that Young did not have a doctorate degree, the former sent him an e-mail to ask if he was interested to take up a Ph.D. degree in Yale, his Alma Mater. His reply was, "Yes, in American studies. But, Yale is out of the question, because university tuition there is too expensive. I cannot go to Yale, because I have a wife and 2 children to support, and a home mortgage to pay."

Another e-mail was sent to Young by Benjamin: "Shawn, I was exactly in your situation, living half-way-around the world in Manila, Philippines, but I still went to Yale. How much more so for an American like you, who are only within a driving distance to New Haven, CT." He answered, "I will try to apply." But, a month later, he changed his mind.

So, Benjamin wrote one more e-mail in a form that Young could understand, a lyric, since that was his field of teaching (and Benjamin's hobby). The result is *SHAWN, YOU DESRVE A YALE DREAM.* But, Benjamin sent it first by e-mail to Dean Jon Butler of Yale Graduate School, whom Benjamin never met, to request if he could consider the song as a theme of his school. The gracious Dean said that he will look into Benjamin's request, and "in the meantime, please convey my best wishes to your Chicago friend, Mr. Young."

51. SHAWN, YOU DESERVE A YALE DREAM
(to Shawn Young; variation of lyric #52)

Don't you ever say, you're too poor
    For your Yale journey as a dreamer
If you've a great idea for the future,
    Yale will find the money to get you there.
Don't you even say, you don't deserve Yale
    It is Yale that deserves someone like you
In its ivied walls, to be trained quite well
    To mentor the scholars of tomorrow

(1) Many young people on earth gladly would
    Trade places with you for being born in
The greatest country in the whole wide world
    It won't be great for you, without a Yale dream.
Don't you ever say, you're too poor
    For your Yale journey as a dreamer
If you've a great idea for the future,
    Yale will find the money to get you there.
Don't you even say, you don't deserve Yale
    It is Yale that deserves someone like you
In its ivied walls, to be trained quite well
    To mentor the scholars of tomorrow

(2) Many young people on earth gladly would
    Trade places with you for being born in
The richest country in the whole wide world
    It won't be rich for you, without a Yale dream.
Don't you ever say, you're too poor
    For your Yale journey as a dreamer
If you've a great idea for the future,
    Yale will find the money to get you there.
Don't you even say, you don't deserve Yale
    It is Yale that deserves someone like you
In its ivied walls, to be trained quite well
    To mentor the scholars of tomorrow

(3) Many young people on earth gladly would
    Trade places with you for being born in
The happiest country in the whole wide world
    It won't be happy for you, without a Yale dream.
Don't you ever say, you're too poor
    For your Yale journey as a dreamer
If you've a great idea for the future,
    Yale will find the money to get you there.
Don't you even say, you don't deserve Yale
    It is Yale that deserves someone like you
In its ivied walls, to be trained quite well
    To mentor the scholars of tomorrow

Lyric #52 titled *YOU'RE NEVER TOO YOUNG TO DREAM* dedicated to Patricia II was specifically written by Benjamin to encourage his co-author when he mentored her for the first time, as the teenage daughter of 2 of his former students at the Newark Adult School.

The song had the positive effect of keeping Patricia II in school, in spite of the fact that she is a single Mom solely taking care of her son, Daniel, and to have a full time job as a waitress in a restaurant as well. Patricia II also acknowledges that "without Benjamin's mentoring her she would not have made it." He helped her with her studies through her first 2 years at Ohlone College in Fremont, CA and eventually through her B.B.A. studies at California State University, East Bay, located in Hayward, CA. It is the hope of both Benjamin and Patricia II that this song will serve as a similar encouragement to our Readers, young and old.

52. YOU'RE NEVER TOO YOUNG TO DREAM
(to Patricia II)

(1) Many young people on earth gladly would
    Trade places with you for residing in
The greatest country in the whole, wide world
    It won't be great for you, without a dream.
    Don't let anyone say that you're too young
        For your journey as a dreamer
    "If you want to build castles on the ground,
        You must first build them in the air!"
    Follow in the footsteps of those who found
        In dreamland, just those need enter
    Who worked really hard when they were still young
        To get the best schooling ever!

(2) Many young people on earth gladly would
    Trade places with you for residing in
The richest country in the whole, wide world
    It won't be rich for you, without a dream.
    Don't let anyone say that you're too young
        For your journey as a dreamer
    "If you want to build castles on the ground,
        You must first build them in the air!"
    Follow in the footsteps of those who found
        In dreamland, just those need enter
    Who worked really hard when they were still young
        To get the best schooling ever!

(3) Many young people on earth gladly would
    Trade places with you for residing in
The happiest country in the whole, wide world
    It won't be happy for you, without a dream.
    Don't let anyone say that you're too young
        For your journey as a dreamer
    "If you want to build castles on the ground,
        You must first build them in the air!"
    Follow in the footsteps of those who found
        In dreamland, just those need enter
    Who worked really hard when they were still young
        To get the best schooling ever!

Conclusion

We conclude with *OPRAH'S ODDS: OBAMA 1, OSAMA O(h)*, dedicated to Oprah Winfrey, host of the most watched American (not just African American) daytime T.V. show, *THE OPRAH WINFREY SHOW.* Her endorsement of the presidential candidacy of Barack Obama, husband of her longtime friend and co-church member in the Trinity United Church in Chicago, Michelle Robinson-Obama, lent early credibility to his presidential candidacy and his eventual unprecedented climb to number 1 position as the nominee of the Democratic Party in this year's federal election.

Like John F. Kennedy, who was the first Catholic, among Protestant presidents in American history, Barack Obama's election will also be the first African American among all Caucasian American presidents. That is most fortuitous at this time, because according to the *USA Today* on July 22, 2008, the continent of Africa happens to be inhabited by people "who most admire Americans." Among the reasons given is that Africa has been the recipient of help from Americans – both public and private – and especially members of the Christian Churches to solve many of its problems, be it genocide, HIV/AIDS, poverty, and so on. Foremost among the American philanthropists is "the most influential evangelist since Billy Graham" Rick Warren, author of *the Purpose-Driven Life* whose principles have been applied to Rwanda, on the request of its President Paul Kagame "the George Washington of Africa" in Warren's own words.

Evidence of the new evangelical attitude towards politics that does not confine their support for Republicans was the invitation extended by Rick Warren in his major conference regarding the HIV/AIDS epidemic in Africa to Democratic Barack Obama to be a speaker.

If Africans have admired Americans up to now, how much more so when we will have an American president who looks like them, Barack Obama, Jr., son of Barack Obama, Sr. from Kenya?

OPRAH'S ODDS: OBAMA 1, OSAMA O(h)
(to Oprah Winfrey; a rhap)

(Echo; 2nd rhappers)

1st rhapper: (1) There's Obama; there's Osama, too.   Obama &
                                                            Osama

                  Don't ever be confused with the two
                  Our "b" stands for brotherhood.   Brotherhood!
                  Their "s" stands for stranglehood.   Stranglehood!
Together: Obama one, Osama o(h)
                       The difference is just a letter
                  But, their Osama is no-can-do
                       Our Obama is a sure winner
                  The reason is quite easy to know
                       Their Osama is a poor loner
                  Our Obama serves both friend and foe
                       And has Oprah as his endorser!

1st rhapper: (2) Love Obama, but hate Osama.   Obama &
                                                            Osama

                  One's good; the other, anathema.
                       Our "b" stands for bravery.   Bravery!
                       Their "s" stands for so scary.   So scary!
Together: Obama one, Osama o(h)
                       The difference is just a letter
                  But, their Osama is no-can-do
                       Our Obama is a sure winner
                  The reason is quite easy to know
                       Their Osama is a poor loner
                  Our Obama serves both friend and foe
                       And has Oprah as his endorser!

1st rhapper: (3) Obama's hip; Osama's passé.   Obama &
                                                            Osama

                  We're the future; they are yesterday.
                       Our "b" stands for beginning.   Beginning!
                       Their "s" stands for stalled stopping.   Stalled
                                                                   stopping!

Together:	Obama one, Osama o(h)
	The difference is just a letter
	But, their Osama is no-can-do
	Our Obama is a sure winner
	The reason is quite easy to know
	Their Osama is a poor loner
	Our Obama serves both friend and foe
	And has Oprah as his endorser!

The final lyric we would like to include in this Conclusion is co-author Patricia II's *WE'RE GUARDIANS OF OBAMASSIMILATION* dedicated to Hillary and other U.S. women. In the future, through intermarriage, Americans will continue to be racially mixed, like Obama, thus *Obamassimilation*. Such a goal is achievable only if we recognize that women are the main instruments of human birth. The few of them who want to work outside the home, such as Hillary, should be rewarded with election to the highest offices including the U.S. presidency.

The *AOL Travel News* listed the top 10 countries in the world where Americans continue to be adored. They are: (a) Albania, (b) Tanzania, (c) India, (d) Vietnam, (e) England, (f) Japan, (g) Ireland, (h) Poland, (i) Ghana, and (j) Canada.

The number 1 test of how much the foregoing American-friendly nations like us is that the favorite heroes' names that they name their children after are (1) Hillary and (2) Bill Clinton!

WE'RE GUARDIANS OF OBAMASSIMILATION
(to Hillary & U.S. women, by Patricia II)

(1) Mestiza sisters:
   Each one is becomin'
As beautiful as us
   By the color of our skin
Mestizas, we're guardians
   Of Obamassimilation
Let's mix blood of Americans
   And rear the next generation!

(2) Mestiza husbands:
    Backbones of our nation,
We need your assistance,
    And full cooperation.
Mestizas, we're guardians
    Of Obamassimilation
Let's mix blood of Americans
    And rear the next generation!

(3) Mestiza mothers:
    Teach our children English.
During their growing years,
    Teach them a second language.
Mestizas, we're guardians
    Of Obamassimilation
Let's mix blood of Americans
    And rear the next generation!

We propose that in "reclaiming the American dream" for the world that future President Barack Obama should revive and rename the John F. Kennedy *PEACE CORPS* to *CAROLINE KENNEDY PEACE CORPS* which emphasizes both continuity and change, as the latter is the only surviving child of the former. We also suggest that the revived body will be headed by Kennedy's own niece and presently California's First Lady Maria Shriver, only fitting as her Dad, Sargent Shriver headed the former.

As a bi-partisan move promised by Obama, and since Maria Shriver's husband, Arnold Schwarzenneger, Republican governor of California has expressed a willingness to be considered for a cabinet post in an Obama government, we think that the most apt initial position for him will be as U.S. ambassador to the United Nations.

Afterword™

The Next B.E.S.T. ™ (Basic Expositions -on- Selected Topics) to be published by iUniverse by Benjamin Franklin Camins will be: *Aung San Suu Kyi: Myanmar's Best Hope*